WINNING WITH PEOPLE

Other books by Michael G. Zey:

The Mentor Connection
The Right Move

WINNING
with
PEOPLE

Building Lifelong Professional
and Personal Success
through the
SUPPORTING CAST PRINCIPLE

MICHAEL G. ZEY, PH.D.

JEREMY P. TARCHER, INC.
Los Angeles

Library of Congress Cataloging in Publication Data

Zey, Michael G.
    Winning with people: building lifelong success through the sup-
    porting cast principle / Michael G. Zey.
        p.   cm.
    ISBN 0-87477-535-3
    1. Interpersonal relations. 2. Success. 3. Success in business.
    I. Title.
    HM132.Z45   1990
    158'.2—dc20   89-27357
                                                                        CIP

Jeremy P. Tarcher, Inc.
5858 Wilshire Blvd.
Suite 200
Los Angeles, California 90036

Distributed by St. Martin's Press, New York

Design by Susan Shankin

Manufactured in the United States of America
10   9   8   7   6   5   4   3   2   1

First Edition

TO CYNTHIA

CONTENTS

ACKNOWLEDGMENTS

I would like to thank the numerous people who supported me during the writing of this book. My editors, Hank Stine and Stephanie Eve Bernstein, provided invaluable insights into the structure and organization of the book. Special thanks go to my publisher, Jeremy Tarcher, for his guidance and encouragement.

To the dozens of people in business and academia who gave their time to be interviewed for this book, thank you! I should also mention my own supporting cast, whose "cheerleading," "celebrating," and advising made the completion of this project much easier—family, friends, colleagues, and of course my agent, Bob Tabian of International Creative Management. Special accolades to Cynthia Zey for her support, including readings and rereadings, of the manuscript.

INTRODUCTION

If you are looking through this book, there are a number of things we can already say about you. First, you're interested in success. You wouldn't even be reading this introduction if you weren't motivated to move ahead in your life. Second, you are probably interested in people, or at least in establishing good relationships. Third, you're probably wondering how to win with people—how to develop the kinds of good relationships that help you achieve your goals.

If the above describes you pretty accurately, you have, as they say, come to the right place. The goal of this book is quite straightforward: to help you achieve solid relationships with the people you know and those you would like to know, so that you will be able to achieve your goals and become more successful.

This is not a book about networking. You will not receive encouragement to telephone strangers or shake the hands of potential "contacts" at professional meetings. The purpose of this book is to help you develop real, permanent, mutually beneficial relationships, both personal and professional, that can lead to true success.

In the book you will explore your friendships, your marriage, and the early relationships in your life, to assess how strong a "supporting cast" you have.

By the time you finish reading this book you should have accomplished several goals. You will:

- Be able to start positive, satisfying relationships, and improve the ones you are already involved in.

- Be more certain of the goals you want to accomplish in both your personal and professional life.

- Know which supporting cast roles are currently unfilled in your life.

- Attain a clear understanding of how others are treating you, and have enhanced insight into the effects they have on your well-being.

- Develop an increased awareness of others' needs.

- Learn how to help others reach their goals.

- Become skilled in differentiating friends from enemies, supporters from saboteurs. (In Chapter 6 you will see how tricky it can be sometimes to tell one from the other.)

- Be able to transform potential enemies into allies.

- Learn how to make your mate, lover, or friend a solid member of your supporting cast.

- Determine whether a prospective mate will support your career and life goals after the honeymoon is over.

- Learn the secrets of retaining loyal members of your supporting cast after you achieve your goals.

- Explore your childhood to determine the extent to which parents, teachers, and early friends helped you on the road to success.

Winning with People is aimed at anyone who is interested in achieving success. It doesn't make any difference what stage of life you are in at present. You may be beginning your career or stuck at your present level; you may be a housewife returning to the job market; or you may be a person who has achieved many of your career goals but who wants to have more satisfying relationships.

As a sociologist, I've spent the better part of the last decade researching success and how to achieve it. Based on this extensive study, I am convinced of one thing: Without the support of others, it is tough, if not impossible, to get to the top. And even if you do, it can get quite lonely up there without a supporting cast.

Consider this the day you will begin to make the positive moves to develop the supporting cast that will help you reach your potential. Make this the day you begin WINNING WITH PEOPLE.

Michael G. Zey, Ph.D.
Somerset, New Jersey
January 1990

CHAPTER ONE

What Every Successful Person Knows

What makes successful people different from average people? Is it talent, intelligence, good looks? Is it where they went to school, how they dress, or how much money they started out with? No, people succeed because they possess an inner knowledge of how the game is really played. Their mastery of this knowledge enables them to achieve their personal and professional goals—and thereby to enhance their lives.

Once you know how to play the game, your ability to succeed will progress by quantum leaps. You will possess essential techniques to achieve whatever you desire, be it money, status, power, or happiness.

High achievers approach their quest for success in a very different way than the ordinary person. Over the course of a decade of researching and interviewing successful people, I have observed a striking trend: that heavy hitters tend to be surrounded by any number of individuals who play substantive roles in their overall success. Because high achievers know how necessary it is to have support in achieving their overall life plan, they have learned how to attract valuable people into their inner circle.

In this book you will learn these vital skills that many high achievers have taken a lifetime to develop—how to identify and attract those individuals who will help you succeed.

What these individuals do to assist the high achiever varies. Some of them are friends who cheer the person on through the darker hours. Others act as advisors and teachers, imparting the inside information needed for success. Others act as personal public relations specialists, spreading the good word about the person's abilities and achievements. Almost all help to build and sustain the individual's self-esteem and self-confidence.

Having loyal allies can definitely help one's career. We hear legends about people whose careers have been saved by their friendships with powerful supporters. An article in *Business Week* described how Steven J. Ross, chairman of Warner Communications, Inc., found out how important the support of a powerful friend can be. In this case, the friend in question is producer-director Steven Spielberg.

In 1987, a powerful contingent of stockholders at Warner opposed Ross's continuation as chairman because they felt that he did not warrant his hefty salary. Spielberg stood up at a shareholders' meeting and threatened to boycott Warner if Ross left. With the threat of Spielberg's taking his talent elsewhere, the anti-Ross faction quickly capitulated. According to Ross, if Spielberg is your supporter, "you can count yourself blessed."

How do high achievers manage to surround themselves with people who will stand up for them as Spielberg did for Ross—supporters dedicated to helping them reach their maximum potential? What do the supporters get in return? When I started my research into this subject in the early 1980s, I had the same questions. In studying dozens of high achievers, it became clear that they had all realized early on that success is synergistic—it happens when people enter into reciprocal relationships in which all members benefit. Throughout their lives these achievers have attracted supporters by correctly determining—and meeting—the needs of those whose assistance they require. They are surrounded by what I have labeled the "supporting cast."

WHAT THE SUPPORTING CAST IS

The supporting cast is a web of interpersonal relationships with people who help you achieve your life goals and to whose personal growth you contribute in return. It is a reciprocal network of friends, acquaintances, and experts, each of whom contributes his or her own special gifts toward your quest for success. In an effective supporting cast you will find people who provide emotional support, building your self-esteem and cheering you on when things seem darkest. Others will help you excel in your job and move up the organizational ladder. The purpose of all the roles these people play is the same—to help you reach your maximum potential.

Throughout the book we will focus on how successful individuals use the supporting cast principles for reaching their goals. From their experiences you will learn how to develop positive, permanent, mutually beneficial relationships, in your personal and professional life, that support your growth in the areas where you need it most. You will find out how high achievers utilize their supporting cast to gain and maintain meaningful success and power.

This book also will show you how the people already in your life—parents, mates, lovers, co-workers, and bosses—affect your success. You will learn what roles these important people are currently playing in your supporting cast, and in which areas you may need assistance.

SYNERGY IS THE KEY TO SUCCESS

In the book *An Empire of Their Own,* Neil Gabler outlines how the early Hollywood movie moguls utilized the supporting cast principle to overcome adversity and establish such giant organizations as Universal Studios and 20th Century-Fox. Even though the Goldwyns, Mayers, and Zukors were on one level competing with one another for the moviegoers' patronage, they also saw themselves as co-pioneers in the fledgling film industry, which itself was competing for the public's entertainment dollar. Acting at times not competitively but cohesively, they helped one another with advice, finances, and the loaning of stars, writers, and directors.

Why should competitors cooperate? The reason is that each recognized that the success of the others was intimately intertwined with their own.

Most high achievers have mastered this principle—that in order to succeed you must enter into cooperative relationships with others. Scientists and philosophers have long understood this.

Anthropologists claim that even the earliest humans, the so-called hominids who date back three to four million years, had to cooperate with one another in order to survive and thrive. Some social scientists claim that the species would probably have disappeared if these early individuals had not learned how to enter into synergistic "win-win" situations with one another. According to sociobiologist Edmund Wilson, cooperation was so critical to the growth of the species that the tendency toward altruistic behavior has become ingrained in the human psyche. Social scientists such as Teilhard de Chardin and Marilyn Ferguson have emphasized that biological and social linkages between individuals play a key role in the continued progress of the human species.

Four Myths about Success

Unfortunately, many of us fail to take the synergy factor into account when we devise our own game plan for achieving success. We are influenced by myths that actually impede, rather than impel, our success.

What are your current assumptions about how people become successful? Why do you think people achieve success in the first place? Let's look at some common misconceptions people have about success.

Myth 1: High achievers must go it alone. One common myth about high achievers is that people who succeed do so completely on their own. But many of the more popular writers on success, even the ones who emphasize such individual activities as positive thinking, imaging, and willpower as methods of achieving goals, maintain that the assistance of others is extremely important for achieving success.

Napoleon Hill, in his best-selling *Think and Grow Rich,* has noted that most of the successful people he researched had gathered around themselves a coterie of individuals who assisted them in achieving their goals. Hill exhorts his readers to attain "perfect harmony" with such an alliance of supporters, and to assure each member of the alliance that his or her needs will also be met in turn. Dr. Irene Kassorla, in *Go for It,* also emphasizes how important it is to be surrounded by people who can help you reach your potential. Her advice is to systematically locate those who can offer advice and assistance, and pursue their help.

The mythology of the great man as lonely genius has been sustained by numerous biographers. But upon closer examination, it becomes clear that achievers like Thomas Edison learned early that true success would not come unless others shared their vision. Even Howard Hughes, the supposed pro- totypical "lone wolf," had his own supporting cast. A recluse from the public, he had a staff of trusted advisors who helped him run his business empire and tended to his personal needs.

Many people fail to appreciate the importance of a sup- porting cast until negative events painfully demonstrate to them how critically they need this group. I have interviewed people who have suffered the consequences of having no one to bolster their confidence, to help them on the job, or to advise them on career or life issues. They may have a mate who refuses to share the household duties. They may have poor job contacts. When they attempt to get support at work for a promotion or a new project, they may find they have few allies.

The point is clear. You achieve your goals not by going it alone, but through the guidance, support, and assistance of others. You bring these people into your supporting cast by meeting their needs. *Synergy* is the key to success.

Myth 2: High achievers are ruthless. Another myth is that in order to succeed, you must compete fiercely with others and overwhelm them—i.e., you can only gain if others lose. This fable is retold by numerous authors who advise people to "look out for number one," to "win by intimidation" in order to "have it all." The message conveyed is that the world is composed of people who can get ahead only by ruthlessly manipulating others to get what they want.

But the research and experience of a plethora of other writers, consultants, and commentators indicate that the world operates very differently. Authors such as Leo Buscaglia, Tom Peters, Mary Kay Ash, and others seem to suggest that caring and cooperation, not ruthlessness, is the optimal way to get people to support your goals. The truly successful people whom I researched and interviewed bear this out. While not always guided by what we might call pure altruism, they are realistic enough to realize that without meeting others' needs they would never meet their own.

To reach your potential, you must do more than look out for number one. Successful people literally take responsibility for the needs of others—mates, co-workers, supporters. Some go so far as to give advice even when it is not directly requested; to provide direction even when it is not solicited; to offer aid even when the person in question doesn't know he needs it.

Typical high achievers have attained their status by recognizing the needs, goals, and feelings of those around them. They are far from ruthless. In fact, they have mastered the art of achieving a high level of synergy with others.

Myth 3: High achievers succeed through talent and skill alone. There is a popular myth that the person who brings to a field or an organization the right combination of education and talent will automatically accomplish his or her goals. While talent and credentials are necessary for success, they are at best prerequisites. People who reach their maximum potential do so through a combination of their own innate talent and their ability to surround themselves with people who can advise them, sponsor them, and serve a variety of other roles, as we will identify throughout this book.

Part of the reason this myth endures is that some entrepreneurs downplay the role that the support of others has played in their success. For example, an article in *Venture* magazine claims that ex-athletes who become successful in business reach their new goals mainly through hard work, knowledge, intelligence, and competitiveness. The article reports that former Minnesota Vikings quarterback Fran Tarkenton credits his success in the software field to hard work. Dave Bing, a Detroit Pistons superstar, links his success in the steel industry to his propensity to take risks. Roger Staubach, the ex-Dallas Cowboys quarterback, presumably became successful in real estate because he learned to be "highly organized and set specific goals."

None seems to refer to the supporting cast principle when describing his success, although this force was undoubtedly operating. In fact, we can assume that the supporting cast was operating so effectively that the individual was able to take it for granted. This notion is supported by tennis player Billie Jean King's explanation of why more women athletes have not enjoyed post-sports success in business careers. She blames the system, which fails to provide a supporting cast to females. According to King, herself successful, an athlete needs mentors to get started in business. She claims that the old-boy network, the ultimate supporting cast, has little interest in female athletes. Making a transition into a new field requires advisors, financiers, technical supporters—the whole array of roles that will be described in the next chapter. Women athletes, regardless of their propensity to take risks and work hard, fail without such a support network.

By gaining others' support the individual becomes more capable of achieving true success and, paradoxically, independence.

Myth 4: High achievers eventually outgrow their need for support. Many of us, even if we accept the idea that high achievers need a supporting cast to achieve initial success, suspect that once they reach their goals they can divest themselves of this group. In fact, nothing could be further from the truth.

As we grow more successful, the need for support *increases.* As we climb the organizational ladder, we need more elaborate and sophisticated forms of support than we did lower down, since our careers and personal lives become even more complex.

High achievers reach their goals because they recognize that regardless of who they are—entrepreneur, artist, corporate executive—the rules, strategies, and tactics needed to succeed stay the same. Success is ultimately dependent on having at hand a supporting cast.

WHAT DOES SUCCESS MEAN TO YOU?

Maintaining a supporting cast is an important technique for attaining success. But what do we mean by this elusive concept, "success"? One point becomes clear from my discussions with respondents: Success means different things to different people.

Of course, many would include in their concept some form of material success. For some, success is clearly and simply the accumulation of money; the stockpiling of wealth in the form of cash, stocks, and bonds becomes the critical object of endeavor. Others focus on what money can buy—a house, a stereo, two vacations a year.

But even in our so-called materialistic society, few people hold such a simplistic definition of success. They may consider anyone who can purchase "all the things money can buy" successful, but few people are willing to settle for this as their only definition of success.

For instance, in addition to a good salary, some people place a high value on career progress—promotions that lead to jobs offering power and status. Many people, too, seek jobs that help them use their capabilities and skills to the fullest. This popular sentiment, that money is not the only measure of success, is reflected in a recent survey in which more than 70 percent of those polled said they would not quit working even if they suddenly came into enough money to enable them to never work again.

For some people, success means striking a balance between a good job and a satisfying home life. Recent surveys have shown that executives are more likely than ever to turn down raises and promotions that are contingent on their moving to another geographic location. Because the lives of their supporting cast—spouse, children, and friends—would be upset by such a move, these executives would rather maintain their social fabric of support and cooperative relationships than take a disruptive step up just for the sake of a promotion.

For some, money and power mean little unless accompanied by respect and popularity. Their main goal in life is to be liked. Others work all their lives to achieve material success, only to realize that what they really want is peace and tranquility. (Occasionally we hear of a former executive now working as a carpenter in some rural village who decided to chuck it all and live a life he finds more satisfying.)

A recent survey appearing in the *Journal of Advertising Research* reported that what people want more than anything else is self-respect. Regardless of how much money they make, people need to feel that what they are doing to make their money is in harmony with their concept of morality.

Ranking up there with self-respect is the desire for a sense of accomplishment. People need to know that what they are doing can have some impact on the world.

Interestingly, what the survey respondents seem to value as much as anything else is satisfying relationships. (The women in the survey ranked this value highest.) As we enter the nineties, there seems to be an increased realization that achieving material goals can be a pretty empty experience unless you have someone with whom to share those rewards.

What are your values? How do you define success? Before you go any farther, think about what you value most. Once you have an insight into your overall value structure, you will be able to assess what types of roles you need filled by your supporting cast.

The Successercize

Throughout this book we will use a tool I have labeled the *Successercize*. It is essentially a quiz or activity list that will help you become more successful. With its help you will be able to assess your current supporting cast, evaluate your close relationships, and review your childhood experiences. Some Successercizes will describe actions you must take to improve your situation on the job. I recommend photocopying the Successercizes rather than writing in the book. That way you'll be able to complete them more than once, or with more than one other person, if the Successercize requires it.

This first Successercize will help you analyze your goals and clarify your own concept of success.

Goal Inventory

In the following Successercize you will evaluate your goals. This is important, since you cannot begin to build your supporting cast effectively until you know what your goals are.

Many of us simultaneously value several different goals. This Successercize will help you think about your priorities and gain insight into which goals you value most.

Use the following key to decide whether each goal is very important, fairly important, only somewhat important, or not essential. Place a "1" in the space next to any goals you consider extremely important, "2" next to the items you consider only fairly important, and so on. Be careful in your responses. If you discover that you have placed a "1" next to every goal, rethink your answers.

1. Extremely important
2. Fairly important
3. Somewhat important
4. Not essential

___ Material goods
___ Warm personal relationships
___ Self-respect
___ Sense of accomplishment
___ Job security
___ Being respected by others

__ Fun/excitement

__ Having a family

__ Independence/autonomy

__ High-status job

__ Physical fitness and health

__ Control over my time

__ Spending time with my children

__ Authority/power

__ Community service

__ Chance to express myself creatively

Next, look at the goals you rated "1," "extremely important." Now rank these goals in relation to one another:

Most important goal _____

Second most important _____

Third most important _____

Fourth most important _____

and so on. Then rank all those goals you rated "2," "fairly
important." This will give you a clearer feeling of what goals
you consider crucial.

Some people resist ranking their goals. Why choose one
goal over another if several are equally appealing? There are
reasons why you should prioritize your goals. For one thing,
you may just not have the time, money, or energy to accomplish all your goals simultaneously. Or another member of
your supporting cast—your mate, for instance—may have

goals that conflict with yours, in which case you have to consider which goals you are willing to compromise or negotiate.
Or your job may force you to choose among several goals.

Keep in mind that your goals may change over time. A
good example of this is the case of Ralph Lauren, the celebrated fashion designer whose company is worth about $2
billion. He is a former tie salesman who has certainly realized
his material dreams.

We tend to think that most "self-made men" are primarily motivated by values such as material gain and power.
But in a *Lear's* magazine article, Lauren readily admitted that
his values have undergone a transformation. A few years ago
he battled meningioma, a tumor arising from the lining
around the brain. After his recovery, he reassessed his life
priorities. His sense of what was truly important had changed.
True, he didn't sell his company and take a trip around the
world. He is too committed to his fashion vision and his
business in general for that. But, as Lauren told an interviewer, "I realize that life can go just like that . . . Don't wait
to tell someone you love them—your wife, your children,
your parents, your girlfriend." Any number of things can
change your goals—from getting married to reaching a mile-
stone birthday, such as 40.

As you begin your exploration of the supporting cast
concept, periodically refer back to your responses on this
Successercize. By keeping in touch with your goals, you will
be better able to determine what roles people in your life
play, and how those roles might be improved.

THE BENEFITS OF A SUPPORTING CAST

What can you realistically expect to accomplish as a result of
all the time and energy expended to recruit these numerous
cast members? Those whom I have interviewed report enor-

mous benefits from this unique support system. Some of these benefits are obvious, some not.

You will accomplish more of your goals. A supporting cast will make it easier for you to meet your goals, whatever they may be. The more you surround yourself with people who fill the roles described in the next chapters, the greater your chances of personal and professional success.

Your self-confidence will improve. Being surrounded by a supporting cast makes it easier for you to believe that you can achieve whatever you desire. As you begin to interact with people who strengthen your self-image, you will find it easier to conceive of yourself as a success. And as your sense of self-esteem grows stronger, you will exude a self-confidence that will attract even more supporters.

Your vistas will expand. People with a solid group of supporters around them also tend to expand the scope of their goals. Once you know that you have people who will help, you begin to believe you can accomplish more. And you can! I have seen many junior executives begin to take on more ambitious projects when they feel they have developed alliances that will come to their assistance when needed.

You will actually become more independent. Paradoxically, the more you work with others to achieve your goals, the greater will be your feeling of autonomy. As you grow in personal power, you will experience an increased sense of freedom of choice and action.

You will have more mutually supportive relationships. Importantly, you will develop lasting relationships built on mutual respect and support. You will be more firmly anchored in a variety of social circles, including family, friends, and organizational and professional networks. These are people who believe in you, who want to help you reach your potential. And similarly you will learn to become their supporter as well.

You will undergo personal growth. Norman Vincent Peale, in *The Power of Positive Thinking,* stated quite emphatically that the act of giving to others actually spurs our own personal growth. "Unless the personality is drawn out of itself and can be of value to someone, it may sicken or die." He speaks of the growth experienced by what he calls the "outgoing, self-giving person." In fact, some scientists claim that the ability to enjoy a longer and happier life may depend on developing these caring relationships. Dr. George L. Maddox, of Duke University's Council on Aging and Human Development, claims that people age best when they have plenty of social contact and live in a supportive, caring environment.

In other words, the act of giving, which is encouraged throughout this book, will benefit you as directly as those to whom you are giving. This fact of mutual benefit is why others will join your supporting cast as well: in synergistic relationships both the giver and the receiver enjoy rewards. Moreover, as you build your supporting cast, you will learn that regardless of what level of success this group of people helps you reach, the act of communicating and sharing with others becomes in and of itself a rewarding experience.

HOW THIS BOOK WILL HELP YOU

By reading this book and completing the Successercizes, you should be better able to build the supporting cast you need to reach your maximum potential.

• You will be given the opportunity to assess your own needs and to determine which roles you need filled in order to become successful.

• You will evaluate those around you. Are the people who make up the total fabric of your life helping you to reach your fullest potential? You will learn some specific measures by which to judge those in your life and determine who your real supporters are.

• You will learn down-to-earth strategies on attracting people to your supporting cast. You will learn the right and wrong ways of getting support, the support turn-ons and turn-offs.

• You will become familiar with the nine basic reasons why people support other people. You will look at the role played by such qualities as charisma and physical appearance in gaining the support of others.

• You will learn how to spot and deal with potential saboteurs who can endanger your career progress. Are there people in your circle who would rather see you fail than succeed? Are co-workers actively seeking to undermine your career? You will explore the reasons why sabotage occurs, both on the job and off, to help you recognize those situations in which needed support may be withheld.

• You will explore your earliest experiences. Did your parents, teachers, and peers encourage, praise, and advise you? Did you have the positive experiences necessary to lay the foundation for success as an adult? You will confront your past—all the experiences and relationships that add up to *you.*

• You will determine the extent to which your mate contributes to, or hinders, your pursuit of your goals. Your spouse or lover is possibly the key cast member. He or she should be someone who boosts your morale, or makes it easier for you to perform your job. Your mate should have a keen desire for you to do well, and should literally see your success as his or her own.

• You will also become familiar with an expanding network of formal supports, the wide variety of specialized services now available. These services—which include everything from child care to grocery shopping, from stress management to personal workout coaches—help round out your support staff with valuable expertise from outside your personal circle.

• Since you succeed to the extent that you can support others, throughout the book you will learn techniques for assessing others' needs and for determining your ability to meet them. You will inventory your own "valuable commodities" (such as special talents, information, or access to power) that you can use to contribute to other people's success.

Even the Loner Needs Support

Occasionally I meet people who are hesitant about adopting a philosophy of interacting with others in order to achieve success. It's not that they disagree with the underlying principle of this book—that one can best further one's career and enhance one's life by establishing alliances. It's just that they do not consider themselves "people-oriented," and hence think that they will be unable to apply the lessons of this book.

This type of person sees himself or herself as something of a loner. Perhaps they greatly value independence or creative solitude. Perhaps they prefer their own company to social interaction. Such people often avoid jobs that involve managing others, networking, or politicking. They may choose jobs that require little social interaction of any kind, neither for the job's day-to-day function nor for career advancement within the specialty.

Are you such a person? At first glance does the "winning with people" approach seem rather foreign? If so, try to keep an open mind. While it is true that you can survive without a supporting cast, you certainly can't achieve all your goals. In other words, without the support of others, you can survive, but not thrive. Moreover, in reality we are all tremendously interdependent on others—whether to obtain our food at the market or to receive our regular paycheck. Many of our daily actions involve the participation of others at some point. Since no one truly goes it alone in today's world, you might as well learn to consciously utilize the human resources around you.

This book should help assuage any fears and apprehensions you may have regarding what's involved in gaining meaningful support from others. Hopefully, by the end of the book you will come to the same conclusion that many successful people have: When it comes to achieving success, both personally and professionally, your best bet is to enlist the help of others. No one can go it alone.

CHAPTER TWO

The Roles People Play

In order to build an effective supporting cast, you first need to have a feel for the variety of support roles that exist. The more you know about the essentials for a supporting cast, the easier it will be for you to create your own.

In my research on high achievers, I studied people receiving a variety of support. Some of these people were famous, some not. But regardless of what sector of society served as the setting for these relationships, and no matter what the social status of the people involved, these individuals had carefully crafted a supporting cast who helped them get to a desired point in life.

What types of roles do the people around you play? Do they give you the support you need to achieve success? Do they cheer you on when you are facing problems? Do they provide advice about your career or life in general? Do they help you celebrate your victories? When you experience failure, do they help you understand why? Are you surrounded by people, on the job or at home, who help build your self-esteem and provide the encouragement you need to go on? Do you have individuals to whom you can turn for financial assistance and advice? On your job, do you have supporters sponsoring you for higher positions?

THE SUPPORTING CAST

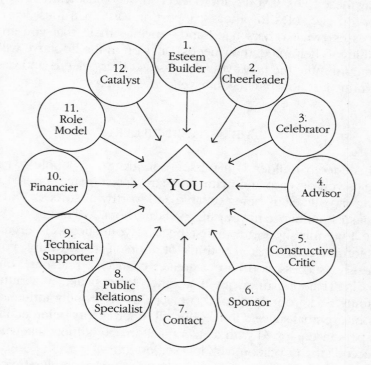

These are just some of the cast member roles we will look at in this chapter. We'll also look at how each type of support makes a unique contribution to your success.

Some roles may be played by several different people; some people may play several roles. In general, the more roles that people around you fill, the greater your chances of achieving success.

At the end of this chapter, Successercize 2: "The Support for Your Life" will help you determine which roles are being fulfilled in your life and what specific individuals are playing those roles.

Keep in mind that it is not enough for you to find people to play these roles. If you want to succeed, you must learn to play appropriate roles in others' supporting casts. You must learn to assess what others need and convince them that you are willing to help meet their needs. Later on in the book we will examine fully the ways you can assess others' needs and determine just how much you have to give others.

THE ESTEEM BUILDER

The esteem builder is a person (or group of people) who helps you develop and maintain a strong self-image, a perception of yourself as being capable and worthy of success. Without such influence in your life, you can't hope to succeed.

I put this support role first, because your success is largely determined by what you think of yourself. If you think you deserve success, you have a greater chance of reaching your goals. That doesn't mean that other factors, like a wealthy family background or good contacts, won't strongly influence your eventual success in life. But, all other factors being equal, a person equipped with a strong self-image is more likely to succeed than a person with low self-esteem.

A strong self-image involves two components. First, you must believe that you can succeed. Second, you must believe that you have *the right to succeed.* You would be surprised at the number of people who reach a certain level of achievement and then falter. Unconsciously they may feel they aren't worthy of success. They are haunted by a sense of inferiority.

What is the source of self-esteem? Our earliest image builders are parents, teachers, and peers who help shape our self-image as a winner or loser. In my interviews, the most successful people have commented that when they were children, their parents and guardians were quick to compliment their ideas and school projects. Most important, the significant others in their lives listened to what they said. It is not surprising that as adults they not only expect to be listened to, they are!

Even as an adult you need to be surrounded by people who believe in your ability to succeed and help to continually reinforce your winning self-concept. You must have friends, colleagues, a lover/mate, and co-workers who ultimately believe in your goals and your ability to meet them.

The stronger your self-image, the more likely you are to get support from others. Self-image can ultimately determine success. In an interview, television personality Ed McMahon once said that one of the reasons he has been so successful is that no matter where he goes, he takes it for granted that he is accepted. Whether he is in front of a major television audience or hobnobbing with political bigwigs, he is convinced he deserves to be there. Since he feels he belongs, others accept him. Those around you quickly sense your feelings of self-worth—or lack of it.

The first step to being accepted and garnering support is to develop the belief that you are as good as the people around you. The person who can walk into any situation exuding an air of self-confidence is light-years ahead of those who feel they don't belong. Self-image has a profound effect on what you think you can accomplish, and therefore on what you do accomplish. This is not a matter of vanity or conceit. People succeed because they are convinced they can.

By the same token, people fail because of a weak self-image, even when they are viewed positively by others. I have witnessed countless extremely talented people whose self-doubt has undermined their attempts to get their just rewards. In the way they act at meetings, the way they deal with subordinates and superiors, they send signals that betray their negative self-perception. Thus, they are overlooked for promotions, omitted from key projects and, ironically, are often outflanked by mediocre people with greater self-confidence.

In order to rebuild your self-image and project a positive self out into the world, you need to bring into your life those whose enthusiasm and respect help stroke your self-esteem. In this book you will learn how to identify esteem builders and cultivate their friendship. You will also develop the ability to identify and deal with those who would subvert your sense of confidence and self-esteem and sabotage your efforts toward success.

People sometimes turn to more formal ego-building agencies, such as therapy and motivation groups, to supplement the assistance they get from friends and family. Chapter 9 will look at the array of services and agencies that can help you build up your sense of self-esteem.

THE CHEERLEADER

The cheerleader is the person who encourages us to succeed and emotionally supports and nurtures us during our setbacks, assuring us that the situation is not as bleak as it seems.

The cheerleader is someone we can turn to in time of trouble. He or she reminds us of our strengths and helps assure us that adversity can be overcome. The cheerleader gives us a sense of perspective that allows us to step away from a situation long enough for panic to subside and our wits to return.

This role is different from esteem building, a long-term process in which a person or group of persons helps us construct a self-image as a competent human being. The cheerleader is someone who helps us feel better about a particular event or gets us through a specific personal crisis.

Who plays the cheerleading role? Many of the women I

interviewed have developed support networks among their women friends who help buttress them during bleaker times. For men and women, a spouse or lover, parent, or sibling may also play this role. In any case, the more successful the person, the greater the chance that there is a cheerleader in his or her life.

Tim and his wife Nancy, young entrepreneurs who own a mail-order business, faced tremendous adversity in their early days. They owed everyone—newspapers in which they had advertised, printers, banks—and for many months were haunted with the feeling that the wolf was at the door.

Nancy became Tim's cheerleader, lifting his spirits when they sagged. If he had any self-doubts that his wife couldn't handle, he always had his brothers. "When things were down, my two closest brothers told me that it was not the end of the world. They were there as cheerleaders," Tim says.

Tim's situation is not unique. Many people, regardless of how strong their other supports, remain plugged in to their family support networks. In spite of years of propaganda about how families instill neuroses and rob people of free-dom and individuality, people still value the intact nuclear family.

Most people realize how important it is to have support outside of the more intimate family relationships as well. They need friends who are available for a quick cheerleading ses-sion. Vicki, an architect, says she has two friends whom she can call at any time for emotional bolstering: "They will always say things like, 'You know you can do it, you will pull through this situation, you always have.' These little pep talks are invaluable."

If you don't receive adequate cheerleading from your inti-mates, perhaps they are not even aware of your needs. Your friends or family may withhold cheerleading not because they are uncaring but because you have given them the impression that you are independent and "without a care in the world." You must make your needs known to those around you. As with all support roles, the more you can convince others that you need help, the more help you will get.

THE CELEBRATOR

The celebrator is another type of positive support akin to the cheerleader. Whereas the cheerleader helps lift our spirits during adversity, the celebrator helps us commemorate the good times. Celebration plays a critical role in our overall success. The people who help celebrate our victories provide the immediate rewards for our accomplishments—rewards that make long-term success seem more worth the effort.

Paulette, one of my respondents, finds it difficult to maintain any real level of success because she lacks supporters to help her celebrate her victories. She recently completed a profitable land deal, for example, but after the deal was closed she celebrated alone. The people surrounding Paulette are quite the opposite of supporters—in many cases they are saboteurs. In fact, she withheld telling them about her deal because past instances led her to suspect that their insecurities, jealousies, and sense of inferiority would cause them to diminish her pleasure.

We all know people who get a raise or promotion, then come home and toast their success alone or with their cat. Success does not guarantee a coterie of well-wishers. But we all need someone to help us celebrate our victories as well as see us through our darker hours. Cynthia, an engineering manager, agrees. "My family always helps me celebrate. Especially my mother and father. My family is big on parties when you're successful."

But Cynthia finds that within her own age group—20 to 25—it is hard to find people who genuinely want to help others celebrate. There is just too much competition these days for some people to develop close friendships.

People who celebrate key events with us give them more meaning. One of my respondents calls celebration "emotional compensation." The psychic benefits of celebration should not be underrated. All the other supports are meaningless if our eventual victories, the goals we have striven for, are celebrated alone.

THE ADVISOR

The advisor is anyone who supplies us with useful information about our jobs, our lives, fields of endeavor, love lives, and especially ourselves. A quick overview of the many activities of this cast member demonstrates how important he or she is to our ultimate success. The advisor may:

- Help you understand the world and your place in it.
- Interpret for you the actions of other people.
- Give you advice on how to proceed in your career.
- Give you insights and knowledge about the political realities of a given organization.
- Generally give you "progress reports" on your life and career.
- Guide you in choosing other supporters.

Early on, parents and educators are only too happy to play this role. Parents are our first advisors and teachers in shaping our values and teaching us about the world.

When she was still a business student in college, Betty (now an executive) had numerous insecurities about entering the business world. One of her greatest uncertainties was how to handle business meetings. She was interning in a major corporation during her senior year, and the company decided to test her management skills by having her present her ideas to a group of vice presidents. Betty turned to her father as an advisor. Since he ran his own business, he was used to presenting proposals and business plans to investors in a formal setting.

Betty's main concerns were that she wouldn't be concise and to the point. She feared she might stumble over her words. "My father told me, 'these people put their pants on one leg at a time, just like you do. You know what you want to say. Don't mince words, just tell them.'"

Her father's advice worked. The corporate vice presidents "actually thought that I was a professional," she says.

But Betty found that as she progressed through her career, The needed to add advisors to her cast. There were just too many questions about the business world, and life in general, that her parents couldn't answer.

In an increasingly complex world, you must continually add new advisors who can help you understand how the world works. There was a time when parents, even grandparents, could play the "wise elder." Today, unless your parents are in the same field or profession you have chosen for yourself, you often must seek life and career advice elsewhere. While parents can provide cheerleading and celebration, the hard core of information increasingly must come from outside the family unit.

In business, we need advisors who can provide us with information that can't be obtained through "official channels." As will be evident throughout the book, those who can utilize informal networks to find out what is really going on within a company will be better off than those who rely on memos and public announcements.

One executive, Alan, mentions that when he was a college senior, one of his friends was an invaluable advisor who helped him get through college successfully. This friend, a

Hispanic, provided Alan with many "street smarts" that helped
him do better in school.

This friend had noticed a certain passivity in Alan that he
felt would limit his ability to function at maximum potential,
especially in the hard-nosed world of management. Alan
explains:

> He taught me how to sell myself. He told me that if you
> want something done, show people that you want it
> done. There is no point in breaking your back to do
> everything. Try to get other people to do it. Get other
> people to help you get to the top.

The advisor is an important component of your supporting cast because he or she helps you interpret the many
events in your life, and especially your career. Many people
think that if they are hired to fill a position, it follows that they
already know all they need to know to perform successfully.
Or if they don't, they can compensate with assistance from
official channels—training sessions, consultants, supervisors.
But this is not always true.

Consider an activity as simple as presenting a proposal.
The formal system may tell you that the right way to go about
the proposal is to write it, present it to the proper committee,
handle rebuttals, and otherwise follow the official channels of
policy-making within the organization.

But the information you receive from an informal advisor
will help you do this task more effectively. The informal advisor will tell you which key players to consult before you
ever put a word on paper. One person can give you a history
of this project. Another can tell you what's really important. So
before you start writing that proposal, you have a wealth of
information that would never have accrued to you without the
advice of your teacher within the organization.

For most of us, a single advisor simply will not do. One
executive, a senior vice president of a health-care company,

refers to this aspect of his supporting cast as his "board of advisors." These advisors, mostly successful individuals who are likewise senior managers, tell him the honest truth about himself and the situations he faces at work. They help him direct important elements of his career.

All things considered, a good teacher/advisor should help you understand what actually makes you happy. How much better off all of us would be if we had someone to help us sort out our priorities. The problem is, few of us realize we need a third party to help us make a connection between what we need and how to get it. In fact, much of this book is devoted to helping you locate and attract people to fill this very role.

You may not realize that there are also unconventional sources of information and advice, such as computerized electronic bulletin boards. Chapter 9 will introduce the ways people are using such novel access to information to better their lives and supplement their supporting casts.

THE CONSTRUCTIVE CRITIC

An important role that many of us need filled is that of constructive critic. While we all need someone who can help us formulate our ideas and give us feedback on our plans, this particular member plays an additional role. The constructive critic actually pokes holes in our arguments and plans to encourage us to come up with better strategies. The person playing this role contributes pieces missing from our own thinking. He may even play devil's advocate, taking a view opposite ours just to help stir our creative juices.

Some of the best support we ever get is constructive criticism. The question is, Can we handle it and will we use it to our best advantage? People who act offended when offered constructive criticism will usually get the desired result—an end to the criticism. But by stifling criticism, they lose the benefit of the creativity of those around them.

If you are a manager—or if you become one—your position of power will probably allow you to stifle criticism. People will fear telling you what you don't want to hear; to protect their own position they will refrain from voicing "negative" remarks, even if in the long run those comments and suggestions would allow you to function more effectively.

In other words, you must let your supporters know that you want and need their energy, ideas, and criticism. You must learn to recognize potential constructive critics and heed their ideas. They help you conceptualize alternative solutions, rethink problems, overcome glitches. They can often spell the difference between your failure and your success.

THE SPONSOR

The sponsor is that member of your supporting cast who helps you get promotions, recommends you for jobs, and personally intercedes in your behalf. While many assume that this role should be filled by a boss or supervisor, you can gather around you any number of sponsors, including professors, executive placement professionals, and business contacts. The sponsor helps you through business school, gets you a raise or promotion, perhaps even prevents you from getting fired.

Given the profound influence sponsors can have on our lives, they can even substitute for parents. In *Fire and Fear,* Jose Torres's biography of heavyweight boxing champion Mike Tyson, we see the power of the sponsor to change the direction of a person's life.

Tyson was the youngest of three children. He lived in the ghettos of Brooklyn, in a world marked by violence and drugs. He ended up in a series of juvenile correctional facilities. While at an upstate New York reformatory, Tyson took up boxing. The camp trainer, impressed with the young man's natural ability, called in trainer Gus D'Amato to hone Tyson's raw physical power. D'Amato not only became Tyson's trainer but also his sponsor. He became a one-man supporting cast, not only turning the youngster into a fighter, but "re-socializing" him. In effect, he helped Tyson make the transition to adulthood.

As useful as sponsors are, this cast member is the most difficult one to locate. In an organization, the people most likely to help you move up the ladder are usually the movers and shakers, those whose success shows that they have already mastered the rules of the game.

We all know powerful people whom we would like to have oversee our development. The trick, of course, is to know how to attract such a person. Throughout this book we will explore methods for identifying these powerful people and attracting their support.

THE CONTACT

Contacts are essential to success. Unlike sponsors, who directly back you and promote you in career and life, the contact is a *connection* to power, a conduit to a better job or to key information. Throughout this book we will be looking at ways to establish valuable contacts.

Contacts are major players in the supporting cast. Ronald, a management consultant to major corporations, must maintain contacts in order to stay in business. In the competitive world of consulting, his liaisons within a company keep feeding him business. Even though he is quality talent, there are many hungry consultants out there eager to take his clients away.

Ronald knows a few people who deliver him good leads, so for the time being he has a fairly lucrative consulting business. But like all consultants, he is fighting an eternal uphill battle. He must maintain his contacts by attending trade association meetings, conferences, and soirees of so-called special-interest groups, in order to keep himself current with real and potential clients.

He realizes that contacts want something in return. It may be referrals of their own. Ronald knows that he must at some point throw them leads to support their own businesses. He explains:

> I think it has to do with being open with people, definitely getting out there, coming across as an expert. People will talk to you because they think you have something for them.

Contacts are the lifeblood of any career. Anyone who has been involved in a job hunt realizes how important it is to maintain a web of contacts. Consultants and others use their pleased customers to lead them to other possible engagements. Entrepreneurs realize that to raise capital to start or expand a business, they need contacts who can lead them to investors.

While you shouldn't be manipulative, to survive and succeed you must be pragmatic. This particular member of your supporting cast may not be a confidant, friend, or even a social acquaintance. Most pure contacts aren't. But they can still play a valuable role in your success.

As you become more successful, some up-and-coming person will probably recruit *you* as a contact. When your assistance is requested later on down the road, just keep in mind how you once benefited from the kindness of strangers.

THE PUBLIC RELATIONS SPECIALIST

Regardless of how well we perform, we will not succeed unless others know about our accomplishments. The public relations specialist helps us gain this needed visibility, both on the job and off. Like other supporting cast members, this person acts on our behalf as an interface between us and the rest of the world.

Most of us do not realize how often and to what extent good publicity has played a role in our achievements throughout our lives. If we recall our early years with any degree of accuracy, we have to admit that parents, relatives, and teachers have often blown our horn for us, bragging to others about our accomplishments.

As we grow older, we are in ever greater need of people who "advertise" our good works. This activity on our behalf is more than an ego boost. Business associates and bosses who spread the good word about us are performing an activity crucial to our overall success. The public relations specialist is involved in what is called impression management (which is discussed at greater length in Chapter 3). Much of our success is built on our ability to convince others that we are already accomplished and talented. This impression is based on a myriad of factors, but what others say about us colors much of what people think of us.

In both work and nonwork situations, your public relations specialist may speak to others about your accomplishments, promote you as a rising star, and tell key players about your abilities. As outsiders relay back to you the positive feedback, this "good press" regarding your accomplishments can only help strengthen your self-image. Others feel good about you, and you begin to accept their positive opinion.

If you commit a major mistake, the way people in your organization interpret your gaffe is ultimately based on their overall impression of you. Are you a basically sound, competent person who made a "one-time" error, or does the mistake confirm suspicions that you are an innately incompetent person who was only waiting to be found out? The p.r. specialist in your supporting cast can help tip the balance of opinion in your favor.

Oddly enough, you may not know about a p.r. specialist's activities in your behalf; you may not even know you have one. A senior executive at AT&T told me that while he assumes someone has been saying positive things about him, he can never be sure who that person is. He assumes that if he is successful and is perceived to be competent and worthy by the bulk of the organization, someone must be speaking in his behalf.

If you suspect that you have a good press agent, it is incumbent upon you to discover this person and establish a dialog. While it is nice to have a secret admirer, there are good reasons to bring this relationship to the surface. In general, it is helpful to know who is behind the scenes pulling strings. You should find out why this person is performing such a valuable service for you. In addition, perhaps you can inform him or her of your other good qualities.

THE TECHNICAL SUPPORTER

The technical supporter can be anyone who helps us in our day-to-day activities. It can be a worker who saves us a few hours by coming to our house. It can be a good, honest mechanic who keeps our car in running order. It can be a day-care center where we bring our children in order to have time to pursue a career. Technical supporters ensure that time constraints won't undermine our efforts to succeed.

Even when all of our emotional and "political" needs are met, we may not succeed unless we also have technical support. Anyone who has witnessed how the absence of such support can upset a day, a week, or a whole career will readily identify with this issue.

Throughout this book you will find quotes from many people who describe the dependency they have developed on various technical support agencies. In Chapter 9, "The Expanding Universe of Formal Supports," you will find useful information on how corporations and private and public organizations provide an increasing range of technical support services.

Members of two-career couples are well aware that technical support is a significant issue in their lives, with direct impact on the careers of both partners. In past generations, women most often played the role of technical supporter: cleaning, preparing meals, bringing up the children, maintaining the house, serving as chief shopper for the family. With most wives and mothers today employed outside the home, the need for technical support is more critical.

Many of my respondents use day care to make their career pursuits easier. Some do it because they cannot survive or maintain a middle-class income without this type of help. Others prefer to pursue their careers, and would rather turn over daily child-care duties to professionals.

Mothers who are pursuing careers at home—as writers, for instance—still need technical support to help maintain the boundary between "career work" and homework. Susan and Michael, a Brooklyn couple, utilize a housekeeper to help with the cleaning and child care. When Susan was working at home as the editor of newsletters for two major magazines, she tried to maintain a physical separation between her career and the daily activity of the household. She set up an office in a remote part of the house, and instructed the housekeeper to interrupt her only in an emergency. The housekeeper, in essence, became a surrogate parent during Susan's writing hours.

The role of technical supporters is growing quite rapidly. Because couples are so busy, they are even recruiting the services of a growing number of personal-services companies that will pay their bills, do their shopping, and provide their meals. Throughout the United States there are companies that will house-sit when the homeowner is away. One company, Odds and Errands, will care for your dog or cat, take in your mail and newspaper, turn your lights on and off—even feed your fish.

Of course, many of these services are expensive. Census data reveal that on average a two-earner family makes only about seven to ten thousand dollars more than a one-earner family. If your payments for technical support eat up the salary increment of the second job, you may want to rethink your career strategies.

THE FINANCIER

This member of your supporting cast may lend you money, invest in your career, or advise you on how to invest or spend your money. Often the financier is not so much a personal associate as an institution or professional: a bank, accountant, lawyer, or investment counselor. On the other hand, a number of may respondents report that mates or family members financially assisted them through the lean years—helped put them through medical school, or paid the bills while they wrote "the great American novel."

Obviously, if you are looking to initiate a business venture, you should know the ins and outs of attracting a financier. Tim felt that he could make money selling dining cards that would guarantee the purchaser a discount on meals at participating restaurants. When starting his company, he looked for financiers. Although Tim and his wife had good jobs, banks would not finance his new venture. Although his credit was good, he had insufficient assets to back up a large business loan.

Tim networked to find an investor, looking for people who wanted a good financial return but could afford to lose their entire stake:

> Most people who are in a solid monetary position are looking for a good financial investment. I gave them the

reasons to invest in my business, showed them a solid
business plan, and made a good case about the return
they would get on their money.

Many of the entrepreneurs I have interviewed, like Tim,
sought financial support from friends. The trick, it seems, is
not to overdo this. Most of my respondents hit their friends
and relatives for the "big loan" only once in their lives, at a
crucial time like completing their education or starting their
own business.

Many people from the upper economic classes regularly
generate financial resources from friends of the same economic group. Many are only too willing to help out one of
"their own." While most of us are not trained to think this way,
it worked for Tim. He explains:

> The initial investor was a friend who received money left
> to him through a trust fund from his grandfather. He
> knew investments, and I showed him my business plan. I
> explained the risks, with no guaranteed results.

Tim also secured a short-term loan from a bank. Before
long he had the money necessary to launch his business.

Again and again we read about the critical role financiers
play in the success of budding entrepreneurs. As reported in
Business Week, two Harvard Business School students, Richard
A. Doyle and George Ligeti, and a University of Chicago graduate, Daniel Kenary, decided to start the Massachusetts Bay
Brewing Company. Bank loans of $300,000 helped. But the
bulk of the startup money—$600,000—came from friends,
family, and classmates who acted collectively and individually
as the group's financiers.

The company is doing well today. Although the trio, in
very un-business school fashion, toil 16 hours a day almost
every day, they now have a product, Harpoon Ale, which is
competing quite well in the New England area.

I wouldn't necessarily advise people to borrow money from friends. But I have found over and over again in my research that people unabashedly do ask friends and relatives for money.

THE ROLE MODEL

The role model is a person with whom we may have minimal contact, if any, but who is an integral member of our supporting cast. This is the person we most want to imitate, whose methods for achieving success we want to copy. We may only watch this person from afar, and in fact the role model may be a media figure, teacher, or relative with whom we have only the remotest of contact. But that person supports us to the extent that he or she contributes to our ultimate self-image and acts as a source of hope even though we may never actively interact.

Many of the people I questioned drew their role models not so much from their personal circle as from real and fictional characters they knew through the electronic and print media. Donald Trump was frequently mentioned by both men and women, a reflection of the enhanced prestige of the entrepreneur in our society. Rock stars such as Bruce Springsteen and TV personalities like Bill Cosby also appear on many people's lists. Ronald Reagan and other politicians also emerge as role models.

There are many reasons why we need role models to achieve success. This cast member provides a viable model of behavior, values, and action that we can try to imitate. Also, the person can serve as a model of how to get support.

Equally important, the role model presents us with irrefutable evidence that success is possible. Many people have begun their climb to success merely by recognizing that others have already made it. Many people who become successful entrepreneurs or executives had parents or close friends with

certain qualities—for example, a propensity to take risks—that
they wanted to emulate.

THE CATALYST

This is one of the more unusual roles that we will encounter.
This is the person who steps into our lives and provides the
necessary spark to help us bring to fruition a project or long-
term goal.

Not everyone has this type of supporter. But you would be
well-advised to seek out such a person. For one thing, a catalyst may provide the psychic energy you need to complete a
project or think through your ideas. It is not so much that they
encourage you; their mere presence, for whatever reason, en-
ergizes you.

Their personality alone may make them good catalysts. I
have heard many a senior executive remark that he keeps
certain staff members around because "we work so well together." What he means is that these associates serve as catalysts in his own creative process.

The positive power of the catalyst is seen most clearly in
the entertainment field. Many legends surround famous creative teams—songwriters such as Rodgers and Hammerstein,
or directors and actors such as Alfred Hitchcock and James
Stewart.

Billy Crystal and Rob Reiner seem to play the catalyst in
each other's creative lives. They met during the 1970s and have
been inseparable since 1976, sharing laughs, angst, even de-
pression. Their relationship has grown over the years, and
expanded even more during the filming of the recent hit
movie *When Harry Met Sally.*

During interviews it is evident how each seems to spark
the innate creativity of the other. Although they were both
successful before they met, they seem to push each other to
greater heights, Reiner as director, Crystal as actor. As Crystal

told *Gentleman's Quarterly,* they are so in sync creatively that they can almost complete each other's sentences, finish each other's thoughts.

Of course, you may feel that you don't need such a "psychic energizer" to accomplish your goals. If you have the right contacts, sponsors, and advisors, someone to provide the necessary thunderbolt to move you to action may seem superfluous. But certainly in the artistic fields, the role of this energizer has been well documented.

KNOW YOUR LIMITATIONS

It is probably clear to you by now that not everyone needs all these roles filled. The trick is to know which ones you most require, and then go after them. If you know your limitations, you are in a good position to know exactly what support you need. In other words, if you are poor at representing yourself, you need a public relations specialist. If you cannot take care of your house or your kids, you need a technical specialist.

This is an important concept in hiring as well. The smart manager hires not employees but supporters. If you are not good at "people skills," hire a supporter who relates well to others. If you are not good at details, get someone who is.

Most successful people I interviewed are well aware of the role that others play in their success, and they are willing to admit it. Most of the senior executives are quite honest about how colleagues, subordinates, and spouses have made their movement up the ladder easier.

EVALUATING YOUR CURRENT SUPPORTING CAST

In reading this chapter you have probably begun to catalog your needs and already have an approximation of the extent to which those needs have or have not been fulfilled. Now that you have a handle on the different types of support necessary to live life successfully, you can begin to evaluate your current support networks. You must honestly assess the people surrounding you. Are they supportive of your efforts, and will they back you when the going gets tough? Which of the above roles do each of these people play in your life?

The following Successercize contains some questions to help you pinpoint what your support needs really are.

The Support for Your Life

In the first part of this Successercize, think of all the people in your personal circle and on your job. If you have any people who fulfill the following roles, answer "yes" to the questions. If not, circle "no."

1. Do the people in your life generally help to build your self-esteem and encourage your positive self-image? Y N

2. Do you have people in your life who help you celebrate when you accomplish your goals? Y N

3. Are there people around you who offer you advice and give you direction on your life and career? Y N

4. Do people in your life offer you encouragement when you are down, and cheer you on when the going gets rough? Y N

5. Do you have people in your circle who will offer you financial help and advice as the need arises? Y N

6. Do you have a sufficient number of technical supporters (child-care providers, cleaning help, etc.) to allow you to pursue career and life goals? Y N

7. Are there those in your circle who perform positive "public relations" for you with people in your field and on the job? Y N

8. Do people in your circle offer you alternative   Y N
   ideas, sometimes even playing devil's advo-
   cate to get you to think through your ideas
   more carefully?

9. Do you have a person (or persons) who   Y N
   provides you the necessary spark, the energy
   you need to go forward and think in new
   directions?

10. Are there people in your company or profes-   Y N
    sion who will sponsor you for positions, raises,
    or promotions?

11. Do you have contacts who can help you get   Y N
    jobs or enter organizations?

12. Are there people, either in your life or whom   Y N
    you see in the media, who provide you useful
    models of behavior, values, and goals?

If you answered each question "yes," you already have a full
supporting cast. If not, the above should give you insight into
which roles you need to have filled.

The second portion of the Successercize is aimed at
helping you assess particular individuals in your circle. For
each person you are evaluating, write in the name of the
person, his or her relationship to you—boss, friend, etc.—and
circle "yes" or "no."

NAME _____

RELATIONSHIP _____

1. Does this person provide you with useful ad-   Y N
   vice about your career or your life?

2. Does this person speak about your good   Y N
   traits or qualities to others, on the job or off?

3. Does this person ever play devil's advocate,   Y N
   offering you criticism where needed?

4. Is this person always ready to help celebrate   Y N
   your victories?

5. Are there times when this person helps you   Y N
   accomplish day-to-day activities, like cleaning
   your house or fixing your car?

6. Does this person generally have a high re-   Y N
   gard for you and actively try to build your
   self-esteem?

7. Has this person ever offered you financial as-   Y N
   sistance or advice?

8. Does this person ever play the catalyst, spark-   Y N
   ing your thinking and providing the energy
   you need to complete projects?

9. Is this person usually supportive when you   Y N
   lose self-confidence or feel down about
   yourself?

10. Has this person ever sponsored you for a   Y N
    promotion or raise, or directly intervened to
    help advance your career?

11. Has this person ever acted as a contact,   Y N
    bringing you together with people who could
    help your actions?

12. Does this person provide you with behaviors   Y N
    and values on which you can model your
    actions?

The more "yes" answers you circled, obviously the more a part of your supporting cast this person is. Of course, no one will play all these roles. And, of course, you may not need them all played.

Your Supporting Cast Must Evolve

You should now have a pretty good idea of your current support needs. Keep in mind, though, that this is not a static picture. As you move through life, your support needs change. At times you may need someone to build your confidence; at other times you may need someone to sponsor you for a position. The important thing is to know what your needs are at any given point. Only in this way can you know what types of people you should recruit into your circle of support.

The rest of this book concentrates on showing you how to attract people into your supporting cast. I hope that by the time you finish this book you will agree with the focal point of the whole exercise: Your success to a great extent is built on others. And if you want others to join your supporting cast, you must be willing to play supporting roles in theirs. That is the secret of gaining true success.

CHAPTER THREE

Why People Support Other People

Why would others want to help you achieve the success you strongly desire and richly deserve? What attracts them to you so that they want to join your supporting cast? Is it fear, sympathy, physical attraction? Does charisma play a role? Or do people support you out of expectation of some gain from the relationship?

In this chapter we will explore the dynamics of interpersonal attraction: the reasons that people might be attracted to you and feel compelled to support you. Until you are familiar with these principles, you will never consistently be able to get the support you need to achieve success and happiness.

THE NINE BASES OF SUPPORT

Successful executives, political leaders, and media figures all seem to realize that it is not enough to know what roles others must play in their lives. They have also discovered some way to attract others into their supporting cast.

These people seem to glide through life, attracting the people they need for attaining their goals. What's their secret? Do they know something about human behavior and motivation that the rest of humanity seems not to be aware of? How are they able to convince others to help them get to the pinnacles of wealth and fame?

What successful people have learned is quite simple: There are certain things other people need, want, and feel compelled to possess, and they will support others who they imagine can fulfill those needs. These underlying motivations are what I call the bases of support, the fundamental reasons why people support other people.

I've had the opportunity to observe the way high government and corporate officials treat their employees, subordinates, members of the press, and the public. They seem to understand that each individual may support them for very different reasons. Everyone seems to be attracted to them, but their motivations are varied.

The basic reasons why people support others, however, are surprisingly limited in number. The following list should give you a feel for the variety of these bases.

THE NINE BASES OF SUPPORT

1. You seem like a winner
2. You have something others want
3. You are charismatic
4. People identify with you
5. You are liked
6. You can be trusted
7. People are altruistic
8. People feel sympathetic toward you
9. People fear you

If you understand these bases and are sensitive to how they operate, you will have little trouble building a supporting cast. You just have to understand which base of support is the prime motivator for each individual you want to recruit into your circle. Some people are motivated by very different bases at different times.

YOU SEEM LIKE A WINNER

No one is better able to build a supporting cast than the person others perceive to be a winner. Why do such people seem to draw cast members so effortlessly? There are several reasons. Some folks think that "winners" have some magic quality that can rub off on them. Others feel more secure about themselves when they deal with successful people rather than mediocre or average individuals. Some people just feel they will look better supporting a winner.

Because this personal characteristic is so critical to attracting a supporting cast, many successful people have worked on developing a winning image, one that makes others confident that working with or under them is the right choice.

What do people see when they encounter you? Do you project the image of a positive, confident winner? If not, there is a lot you can do to change your image. If you need some motivation to change your public persona, just remember that the more others perceive you to be truly ahead of the game, the greater the likelihood that they will support you.

Mastering the Art of Impression Management

Even if you are the most competent, talented, and creative individual, there is no guarantee that others will view you as a winner. If people don't *feel* that you are competent, they may develop many negative concepts about you and your ability.

How do you go about shedding this false image? Many of my respondents are quite practiced in what social scientists call impression management, the art of controlling the perceptions that others have of them.

To start, think about the overall impression you make. Is it one of a victim or loser? This image will do nothing to gain support. People like to deal with individuals who seem to be on top of their lives and ahead of the game, people who control situations rather than allowing people and events to control them.

Here are some quick pointers on developing a winning image.

Operate at your highest performance level. In order to win support, you have to be better than good. Be excellent in every task, from the most trivial to the most significant. If you are satisfied with being just average, the people around you will figure, "why bother?"

To operate at highest efficiency, you have to take a broad view of your job. Be adaptable! This means that you should try to transcend your specialty, whether it be marketing, science, engineering, sales, or personnel. Until it becomes apparent to the powers that be that you can make a broader contribution to the organizational mission, you will be seen as a specialist limited in your ability to contribute to the company's overall progress.

If, for instance, you serve on an interdisciplinary task force, or initiate a project that incorporates many different specialties, the higher-ups will quickly see that you have a broader view of the organization and can transcend your own area of expertise. Says one executive, "I haven't seen anyone with a demonstrated higher skill denied an opportunity to move up. But I have seen many who have stayed within their narrow specialty who have stagnated."

Many people have a profound understanding of the inner workings of the computer, for example, but when it comes to describing how the computer fits into the overall company scheme, they are lost. Employees like this will never move up, because they never exhibit real leadership. It becomes the task of the generalist to integrate that computer into the overall scheme of the organization. To the generalist goes the power.

Demonstrate organizational savvy. It is not just in the areas of job performance and technical knowledge that you should demonstrate your capacity for excellence. Superiors and subordinates in any corporation or institution will support the individual who exhibits organizational savvy—an innate understanding of the corporate culture and its values, proprieties, and priorities. Who wouldn't want to support someone who shows he has a feel for the right way of doing things? Senior managers especially watch to see which junior members are able to interact smoothly with fellow workers.

Many executives complain that it is hard to find employees who know how to avoid stepping on others' toes, insulting higher-ups, or creating embarrassments for the company and boss. Develop corporate "street smarts" and you will have no problem attracting supporters.

Look eager, but not hungry. Since people support someone who looks like a winner, you must not emit obvious signals that you are in need of help. The people who seem to need help the least tend to attract it the most.

Ronald, the successful management consultant mentioned in Chapter 2, advises against coming across as vulnerable. In business most people don't want to deal with someone who seems desperate, he says, because they think there's something wrong with him.

Similarly, many of my respondents betray an almost superstitious belief that others' bad luck can rub off on them. Fortunately, they feel the same way about winners' good luck.

Talk about your strengths, not your weaknesses. One of the surest ways of discouraging support is to emphasize your shortcomings to others. You may feel insecure about your abilities, you may worry about the future, or you may imagine dangers in your life or your job. While you may openly discuss your shortcomings with a mate, a close friend, or a therapist, be careful in selecting who you discuss your weaknesses with. Even if the listener expresses sympathy, your confession may undermine that person's confidence in you.

Emphasize the positive. It is human nature to want to hear good things. Very often people's own insecurities make them avoid those they perceive as losers. Start complaining to everyone, and you lose everyone's support.

That does not mean that you can't express your dissatisfactions, only that you have to choose carefully those with whom you commiserate. Once you have someone in your camp as a mentor or advisor, you can be more open with him or her about your problems.

How do you decide on the right person (or persons) with whom you can expose your weaknesses? Obviously, someone not related to your work, like a mate or outside friend, could serve as a sounding board for your problems. You may even choose to throw tantrums or otherwise vent your anger in front of these people.

But in a work situation, be extremely careful about when and in front of whom you express fears or insecurities. Potential saboteurs can easily take advantage of you in your weaker moments. People who trust and rely upon you may begin to lose faith in you if they perceive you as weak. You must use your judgment, and consider how a given individual will perceive your negative behaviors.

Your goal is to establish an ambiance of competence around yourself. Of course you are the best manager, the best writer, the best financial analyst. If you want to establish a winning image, people must have no doubt you are the best.

Impress without intimidating. The people who are most apt to garner support are the very people who appear to want power the least. They have learned that to become successful they must not threaten those whose support they need.

Let me give you an example. On a consulting assignment with the United States Postal Service, I met an assistant post-master general who exercised considerable control over people, budgets, and resources. I expected such a man to be a high-powered, aggressive type. Instead I discovered that he was one of the most unassuming individuals I had ever met. I began to realize why he had the support of everyone in the organization: While he exuded an inner strength that spoke of control and power, he was at the same time unintimidating.

This man, like many others in his position, gets the support and cooperation of others because people believe that he wants to serve, not to gain power. That is the secret of not intimidating others. Many highly placed people seem not to need power or want authority. In fact, the demeanor of many high-powered executives seems unpretentious and, more important, nonthreatening.

YOU HAVE SOMETHING OTHERS WANT

Executives and politicians alike have learned one basic lesson about garnering support, whether it be the loyalty of employees or the votes of constituents: People support others out of their own self-interest. If you want to become successful, you must be perceived as serving others' needs. Simply put, people will support you if they think you have something they want.

You must determine what commodities you possess that can be exchanged with potential allies and supporters. Let's take a quick look at what others need and what you have to offer. (In Chapter 8 we will make a more systematic assessment.)

Through your contacts, you might be able to provide a job for someone. You might have extra money to lend or give. You may have knowledge or expertise that others value. If you are securely placed within an organization, you may provide a linkage to powerful and influential people there. On the job, fellow employees may support you because they think you are a star, or about to become one; hence it is beneficial to them to hook up with you.

Money, power, status—these are all barterable items that can become bases of support. But how do people know that you are someone who can deliver the goods? Certain characteristics immediately signal to others that you may be in a position to help them achieve their goals.

Your level of ambition is one such trait. You might think that exhibiting ambition would tend to scare those around you and actually detract from support. But there is something innately attractive about people who exhibit this quality. Your ambition signifies to others that you are worthy of their support, because you are apt to become successful if for no other reason than the fact that you want to. Senior executives, for instance, like ambitious junior members of the organization. The ambitious are willing to work hard, are serious about their jobs, and are quality performers.

Another signal that you can fulfill others' needs is your willingness to take responsibility for your actions. Whether in business or in your personal life, you will quickly discover that taking responsibility (and blame when necessary) for your actions is a trait highly regarded by others. They assume that if you are willing to accept risks, you must be capable of handling responsibility. The more competent they perceive you to be, the more they believe in your ability to be able to help them achieve their goals.

Acceptance of responsibility often expresses itself as a tendency to initiate projects, to take action on one's own—in effect, to lead. Senior members of organizations value a person who is willing to share responsibility and possibly assume some of the senior person's work load.

Cynthia, a young engineer, built her supporting cast in large part by developing and exercising this trait. "My boss from day one told me he wanted someone he could depend on, give assignments to, and trust to carry them out," she says. As she helped her boss do his job, he eventually reciprocated by promoting her.

Another trait that suggests to others that you can deliver power and status is your commitment to the organization. This is true whether you are in the arts, business, academia, or sports. Your manifest long-term commitment to the organization will draw support from senior executives and others in power. Since they see their own lives and futures closely tied to the fortunes of their company, they are likely to support you if they perceive that you are committed to helping the company grow.

According to one executive, people who are committed to making a contribution are the people who are most likely to get his attention.

> The thing I look for are people who are willing to commit as much to the company as they are looking for the company to commit to them. They are not just looking for me or somebody to knock on the door and say, "Your brass ring has arrived."

What commodities do you have that others need to achieve their own goals? Do people know about them? Throughout the book we will look at how you can first identify what others want from you, and then convince them that you can in fact deliver what they need.

YOU ARE CHARISMATIC

While people may differ in their definition of charisma, most agree it is a surefire trait for attracting others' support. Charisma, by its very nature, attracts. People who have charisma are what I call superattractors. You know them when you see them: they just have a certain quality others want to latch onto. According to Pat Buchanan in his recent autobiography, John F. Kennedy had charisma. Buchanan relates how Kennedy could walk into a room and command attention from both men and women. Some attributed this to the aura of money and the Kennedy name. But many richer people in no way rivaled the level of attraction Kennedy could command.

The character portrayed in the movie *Tucker* possessed a certain charisma. Tucker, an automotive innovator of the late 1940s, was determined to develop a car with safety features and fuel economy unheard of at the time. He had to buck the big three automakers in his quest, and he needed all the support he could muster. Even in the darkest days of his enterprise, his personal magnetism and determination helped him wrestle money from financiers and command loyalty from his employees.

An executive at Johnson & Johnson describes how, when his chairman enters the room, all eyes focus on him. Is it just his position in the firm that commands attention? This manager doesn't think so. The chairman, while making others feel right at home, leaves no doubt that he is the "chairman of something." His mere presence suggests power and ability.

Natural attractiveness won't replace competence, but it can help you perform in many higher-level positions. The inner

glow of a charismatic personality can sometimes draw potential supporters. Each accomplishment tends to enhance (and
sometimes even creates) the aura of power and ability that we
call charisma.

What Charisma Really Is

While charisma is often described in ethereal, almost mystical
terms, all "charismatic" individuals share a combination of
characteristics—including energy, creativity, intelligence, and
vision—that add up to the spark others find so attractive.

Why is energy so important here? People generally associate vitality and energy with youth, vigor, new ideas, and inno-
vation. Hence, a high energy level tells people that you are a
mover and a shaker. Those around you can only benefit by
being connected to a person who accomplishes things vig-
orously and quickly.

Creativity is a charismatic trait because people support
those who introduce new ideas. Creativity implies the ability
to get projects moving. Innovative people are seen as problem
solvers. Notice how positively people react to the person who
discovers the answer to a problem everyone else has been
unable to solve.

Keep in mind, however, that the more creative you are, the
more connected you must be to others on a social and human
level. Witness the bad publicity surrounding those current
geniuses, the "computer nerds." They are often viewed as
aloof and hence somewhat dangerous, what with the threat
of computer "viruses" and other misuses of technology. You
must show that your creativity is connected to solving problems for people.

Intelligence is a charismatic trait because it signifies mastery. As work and society become more complex, people will
be increasingly attracted to this quality.

Of course, there are many types of intelligence. We see one type exhibited on the television game show "Jeopardy": vast knowledge and quick recall. But there are others, such as analytic thinking, logic, and, of course, wisdom. In business, intelligence often means the ability to analyze a problem quickly and identify the relevant elements. But keep in mind that intelligence can both attract and repel. Nobody likes the arrogant "intellectual." People want to know that your wisdom can help them, not serve as a way for you to belittle them.

In essence, we see others as charismatic because they seem to represent a higher level of development or accomplishment. We sense that they have already reached a stage toward which we are straining—personally, intellectually, or professionally.

If people perceive you as having reached this higher level, they may see you as charismatic and worthy of support. People always secretly hope that charisma will rub off on them, like magic dust.

You should keep this source of attraction in mind when you are in a supervisory position. People will reach out to you to gain your knowledge, experience, and competence. Since people who are struggling at lower levels usually want to move up, they are drawn, sometimes unconsciously, to those who seem to be more advanced.

Robert Wright, president of General Electric Financial Services division, reportedly moved up quickly at GE because he "caught his superiors' eyes." What was it that made them support and promote him? According to *Forbes* magazine, senior managers were attracted to Wright because of his vision—his ability to see where the company should go—and his ability to push it in that direction.

Even those senior to you will be drawn to you if you are charismatic, regardless of how far ahead of you they are in the organization. This dynamic very often envelops the relationship between an older executive, professor, or mentor and a younger person.

Many of the successful people I interviewed mentioned that charismatic types exude a quiet confidence that subtly suggests self-control and hence control over situations. It is this quality that makes others feel that supporting the charismatic person will help them meet their own goals.

Can Charisma Be Developed?

Although you don't need charisma in order to develop a supporting cast, it doesn't hurt. Can you develop this quality, or do you have to be lucky enough to be born with it? There is much you can do to develop a more charismatic image, to become a superattractor.

For one thing, you can try to increase your energy level. You may be under the impression that one is either blessed with a high energy level or forced to act, move, and think at a slower pace. But energy is more mental than physical.

One executive keeps his energy level up by surrounding himself with younger people. He competes in sports and, like so many others today, refuses to accept the idea that numerical age means being "aged."

The more youthful you are, the more people will assume that you have something on the ball. After age 30, a differentiation begins to occur among people. Many start to think of themselves as "older," become nostalgic for their youth (real and assumed), and become alienated from the younger generation of people and ideas.

A person who wants to be perceived as charismatic must be considered "current." You cannot attract the support of people from whom you are at heart alienated. In the words of one executive:

My mind-set is such that someone has to remind me of
my age. I don't think of myself as 40-plus. Some young
woman on my company volleyball team mentioned when
she heard my age, "You're old enough to be my dad." I
just ignored her comment and continued to play.

Much of age is psychological. You will have a better
chance of retaining a high energy level if you don't accept the
opinions of those around you about how you are supposed to
slow down as you get older. Pianist Vladimir Horowitz, for
example, toured the world well into his nineties. He knew that
if he stopped performing he would probably go into physical
decline. He refused to accept the conventional social limits
of age.
    Can charisma be taught? Lisa, a public relations director
whom I interviewed, claims that people can be coached to
become more charismatic. Many corporate vice presidents receive instruction in how to make interesting presentations and
give rousing speeches—everything from hand motions to
voice inflection. If you want to appear charismatic, work on
your presentation style.
    Presidential candidates today are surrounded by a coterie
of media consultants who advise them on how to "communicate." What they really teach is how to exude a range of
"magic" qualities—control, wisdom, concern.
    Charisma will win additional support. But as we see in
many political situations, charisma can only go so far. A presi-
dential candidate may be able to exude charisma to crowds
who see him for single, brief appearances. But many a candidate has discovered that the effects of charisma can diminish
as the press and the public scrutinize his programs and ideas.
Charismatic or not, in the long run you have to meet expectations of performance and competence.
    If you don't have charisma, don't worry. Most people who
attract support do so by understanding others' needs as well

as their own. Developing support takes practice. Charisma is only one of many tools.

PEOPLE IDENTIFY WITH YOU

You may not realize that others are often motivated to help you simply because they see something of themselves in you. By recognizing situations in which others identify with you, you can transform that identification into meaningful support.

In studying the mentoring phenomenon for several years, I have found that one of the reasons people choose this often arduous task is that they see much of themselves in the protégé. A certain warmth, friendliness, and familiarity seem to emerge early in some relationships with bosses, subordinates, and acquaintances. Often this is because those involved recognize themselves in one another.

The process is subtle. Some think there is more than a small amount of narcissism at work here. The mentor subconsciously affirms his or her own worth by supporting someone seen to be similar in personality, values, looks, even social background.

Is the senior person trying to establish a beachhead in the organization for "his type of person," one who shares his values, personality, and interests? Does he think the world would be a better place with more of "his kind" in positions of power? Whatever the motivation, the person who identifies with you can easily be convinced to support your quest for success.

YOU ARE LIKED

Some people acquire supporting cast members because they have personal charm and a pleasing personality. Of course, charm is not enough to build a true supporting cast. But in many organizations it is important to be likable in order to succeed and garner support.

You don't have to be charismatic to be liked, and that is why I consider this a separate base of support. There are many qualities that can make someone likable: looks, a sense of humor, and most important (at least in a business/organizational environment), cooperativeness.

The ability to get along with others is an important component of acquiring support. The image of the maverick, the lone cowboy, the test pilot flying solo among the clouds, holds a proud position in our culture. However, while people respect individualistic thinking and uniqueness, at heart they distrust the lone wolf or the complete individualist.

Business uses the concept of the "team player" to capture that spirit of cooperativeness. The team player knows what is good for the group and works in that direction. If you are perceived as a team player, you will be liked and receive support. You are sending people the signal that you are in fact interested in helping them meet their goals.

This doesn't mean that to get ahead you must give up your independence. All teams have their grunts, their offensive linemen, but they also have their quarterback. Just because one of the rules of the game is that you must be a team player, you don't have to relinquish your ambition to be the chief signal caller. You can do both. Just remember that you need the support of the whole team to succeed.

A quarterback on one National Football League team claims that every Sunday night after a win, he takes to dinner his offensive front linemen, the people who protect him from opposing players. This is by no means a cheap dinner—280-pound linemen have quite an appetite, especially after playing three hours of football. But this quarterback feels it is worth the price to show appreciation to these gargantuan members of his supporting cast.

By the same token, the loner will always have problems attracting support. You may think that you are impressing a boss by appearing to be a maverick. But many supervisors and managers are threatened by this type of person. In the long run, you are making others feel that they are not valuable, that you don't need their skills. According to one manager:

> Managers really look for the person who is not on an ego trip, who is not one of these "I can do it all" types. . . . This type of person may win the isolated project. But they will never really move up the ladder because they have not demonstrated the ability to work with peers, for superiors, and to work well with subordinates.

One senior vice president of human resources claims that because lone wolves haven't shown an ability to work cooperatively with people, most reach a point where they can't move up. The ability to work well with others, at any level of the company, as well as the ability to garner support and establish linkages—in essence, to make people like you—is in itself a prerequisite for promotion.

YOU CAN BE TRUSTED

People in power will often support a person who they believe will keep their secrets, remain loyal, and not betray them to their enemies.

Whether in life or on the job, there is no better way to gain a supporting cast member than establishing a pattern of loyalty toward that person. Your action may be as simple as keeping someone's secret, or standing by a superior or subordinate under fire.

Not only does trustworthiness motivate the person directly involved to support you, but those witnessing your display of loyalty will also be more prone to become a part of your supporting cast.

Many of my respondents were able to build a steadfast supporting cast of confidants, advisors, and public relations specialists by demonstrating loyalty in some critical situation.

PEOPLE ARE ALTRUISTIC

Occasionally you may be lucky enough to encounter people who support others simply because it makes them feel good to do so. This is a far more common occurrence than you might imagine. When I studied mentors for my book *The Mentor Connection,* I met many people who supported others almost exclusively out of altruism. They enjoyed playing the role of wise elder. Having accomplished their own goals, they were ready to pass on the reins to younger persons.

Social psychologist Erik Erikson labeled this tendency "generativity." He believed that individuals who have achieved what they've desired in life try to give back something to society in return by helping newcomers.

You will probably hear about people in your organization who have earned a reputation for nurturing up-and-coming talent. These altruistic individuals are viewed as making a real contribution to the growth of the organization. Because such people truly feel gratified by helping others, you should not hesitate to ask for their support when you need it. Of course, you don't want to overwhelm potential supporters with requests, but you can increase your chances of getting support by simply asking for it. The protégé role, if played properly, can serve as a useful means for gathering support.

PEOPLE FEEL SYMPATHETIC TOWARD YOU

When I was a student I had a friend who had trouble with the work in many courses. But he had devised an innovative way of negotiating his way through school: he related an elaborate hard-luck story to each professor. As smart as these academics were, they fell for my friends tales of hardship and charitably gave him passing grades.

Yes, some people do get support because they are so incompetent that others feel compelled to help. Although you may be tempted to exploit this base of support, your "successful" results will be strictly short-term. In the long run, the sympathy strategy will backfire.

People support other people because they see themselves receiving something positive in return. In an increasingly competitive world, the incompetent individual is as likely to be victimized as supported. Occasionally, someone may catch you when you fall backward, but dont count on them to help you up.

It is unpleasant to watch an individual who has come to depend on sympathy as a method of garnering support. What works for us as children can fail us miserably as we move into the adult world.

PEOPLE FEAR YOU

In certain situations people may support an individual for no other reason than fear: they feel it is safer to support this person than not. We have all seen situations on the job or in our personal life where someone gains support out of fear. Let me warn you that this type of support is fraught with danger. As soon as the "supporters" sense weakness, their support will turn to sabotage.

Many of the executives I interviewed are emphatic in their denunciation of fear as a method of gaining support. While you may exact acquiescence from employees by using fear tactics, says one executive, "This isn't real support. They could be stabbing you behind your back. It's public support, but are they just doing it because their job is at stake?"

At best, fear will get you only the bare minimum effort out of subordinates. If you need employees to give you something extra, like staying overtime or working on a holiday, fear can't compare to other support bases, such as trust or charisma, for getting the support you need.

It should be obvious by now that you will gain support by meeting some need, conscious or unconscious, in others. We will look at this issue in depth in Chapter 8, "Joining Another's Supporting Cast." In terms of developing your own supporting cast, your goal should be to discover what others want, what sorts of things will motivate them to help you—in other words, what bases of support are at play in your relationships.

LOOKING GOOD

Do you believe that the better looking you are, the more support you will garner? Do you think that the more expensively you are dressed, the more people will be attracted to you on the job? Will controlling your weight lead to a promotion? Do good looks at least give you a running start in life and on the job?

There is no doubt that physical presentation of self is an important component of attracting the people who will help you succeed. In a recent study of how boards of directors choose their CEOs, "physical attractiveness" was mentioned as a criterion (along with a plethora of other more bottom-line traits). In controlled laboratory situations as well, subjects repeatedly demonstrate their propensity to attribute to people they consider physically attractive a whole range of other positive characteristics, including intelligence, success, and wealth.

The concept of attractiveness is elusive and complex. In a recent *Self* magazine article, Michael Korda claims that a quick perusal of the photos of Fortune 500 CEOs would reveal that handsomeness is not a uniform requirement for corporate superstardom. But later in the article he mentions that physical fitness and neatness in dress, while they won't substitute for competence, play a role in success.

Many people try to improve their appearance by purchasing expensive wardrobes, coloring their hair, or undergoing cosmetic surgery. One East Coast plastic surgeon claims that one-third of his patients are male executives. Most of those who undergo operations to eliminate wrinkles and turn back the signs of aging will claim they are doing so for personal, not business, reasons. But interviews reveal the deep-seated insecurities that motivate many of them. Their actions betray a belief that the younger looking one is, the greater one's ability to attract supporters and become successful on the job.

Change What You Can, Don't Worry about the Rest

Many bosses go to great lengths in their attempts to improve subordinates' appearances. They truly believe that how the "product" is packaged can be an enhancer or a barrier to success. Are there aspects of your appearance that need improvement? What part of your physical appearance would you change if you could?

One executive in a major pharmaceutical firm claims that achieving at least a passable appearance can increase chances for career success. "You can take someone who is not pleasing to the eye and bring them to the point where their looks are not distracting to their performance. You can neutralize the negative."

How much can you actually change? While you can't turn an "ugly duckling into a swan," as one executive puts it, you can certainly improve your personal hygiene. You can try to remember to smile more often.

Several successful people claim that maintaining your health can help build others' confidence in you. People associate good health with competence, capability, and self-control.

We may subconsciously blame the victim of sickness for his or her condition; we may believe that to some extent, people who get sick must have let themselves get run down.

Weight is another critical variable. For some people in positions of power, overweight signifies a person who is out of control. People will support those whom they perceive as being in control—of themselves as well as of external factors.

Dress the Part

Dress (and its ancillary concept, neatness) is a key in impression management. Much has been written about the relationship of dress to gaining support from others. *Dress for Success* author John Molloy has influenced a generation of careers with his tips and philosophy.

Dressing inappropriately on the job can hurt you. One of my respondents claims that dressing like the pictures in *GQ* magazine won't help in some of the more "dress-down" middle-class corporations. In many companies, "elegance" in apparel is considered superficial, Michael Korda says, while "sharpness" in dress is highly valued.

In organizations, the dress style of people in power is often emulated by everyone else. If the general manager or president starts to take off his jacket at lunch in the cafeteria, soon everyone is in shirtsleeves.

The simple rule of thumb regarding appearance is: Know your environment. In your organization, if quality in clothes counts, if spending money on your wardrobe seems to be an important symbolic gesture, then you must conform in order to gather support.

You can change people's perceptions of you by changing your dress style. Many executives claim that the quickest way to attract support from above in any company is to look like you actually belong at a higher level of the organization. As you begin to conform to this "dress one level up" style, the higher-ups' perceptions of you change subtly. They begin to see you as a potential peer, as a person who fits in.

It's not as though they say to themselves, "Johnny is dressing differently—he is more important than I originally thought." But when they later make promotional decisions or become your advisor, your image as "one of them" will stick in their minds. It gives you an added advantage.

The unspoken messages that you send out about yourself are critical in attracting support. They subconsciously work in tandem with your other good qualities. One senior vice president admits he is influenced by the power of dress:

> I'm not sure I consciously say about a person, "He looks like one of me." But you start forming images in your mind about the person. You like their ability, and if in addition you have this subliminal thought about this individual, that their image is good, it can't hurt.

In some organizations, higher levels don't mean dressing differently. As one executive told me, "My president wears cheap suits like I do." But you wouldn't adopt that style in a prestigious law firm where everyone dresses well. In academia, however, dressing too formally is perceived by many senior professors as pretentious. You will never gather their support by dressing better than they do. Remember your environment, and dress for the part you'd like to play in it.

To learn how to dress the part, observe people in power in your organization, or consult peers, advisors, or the corporate grapevine. If you have some extra money, hire a fashion consultant or color coordinator.

If the whole idea of dressing the part makes you uncomfortable, perhaps it's because the organization to which you are affiliated makes you uncomfortable. If you don't seem to belong where you are, you won't get support. Consider whether you may be working in the wrong organization.

Although we have been concentrating on dress in business, remember that dress is an important attractor in any situation. The whole sexual attraction game is permeated with a variety of dress codes. The better dressed you are, the more attention you will get, whether from the CEO or the opposite sex or the mechanic fixing your car.

THE SUBLIMINAL SIDE OF SUPPORT

In a meeting, you find yourself running into resistance. In a job interview, you emerge an hour later with the feeling that somehow the interviewer didn't like you. At a party, you find that another guest you spoke to politely became brusque. What happened? Where did you go wrong?

Support is not always a clear exchange system that you can easily negotiate by offering favors in return for favors. Gaining support is a complex process, with more than a trace of the subliminal. People sometimes offer or withdraw support for fairly irrational reasons. They may not even know why they feel the way they do about you.

While many of us deny this unpleasant aspect of interpersonal dynamics, it is nonetheless a potent source of both power and problems. For instance, a person may support or reject you simply because you remind him of someone else: his mother, for instance, or the girl who would never date him, or the son who rejected him. Any number of physical attributes or mannerisms can trigger such a reaction.

Some people try to use similar associative factors in their favor. Political consultants are always attempting to transform their clients' images to exploit the subliminal aspects of support. They try to make a candidate look a certain way: young, wise, graceful, "all-American." They know that people often subconsciously vote on the basis of highly personalized traits that have very little to do with who the candidate is or what he stands for.

Unfortunately, there is little you can do to control such subliminal aspects of the impression you make. You can control your dress style, you can behave like a winner, and you may even possess many of the commodities (such as talent or knowledge) that the other person desperately needs. But he still might withhold support because you remind him of his ex-wife.

While you can't control this particular variable, you can certainly take it into consideration when personality clashes or sabotage occur. If it seems that a conflict is brewing, go with your "sixth sense" and withdraw. Such a person will never join your supporting cast.

On the other hand, be sure to be sensitive to those situations in which the subliminal factors work in your favor. You never know when potential supporters unconsciously perceive you as someone they like—a son, a lover, or a trusted friend.

INCREASING EXPOSURE

As obvious as it sounds, people support other people only when they are aware that they exist. Without some degree of exposure, your chances of gaining support are nil. In Chapter 5 we will deal at length with the issue of how to gain visibility in your work organization. Here we will briefly introduce some ideas on how you can become more visible in your daily life.

Be Resourceful in Networking

It's important that you use social networking to attract others. People in the entertainment, writing, and acting fields are well aware of this means of moving ahead. A writer I know, who was conducting research for a book, attended a swank New York party in hopes of meeting some celebrities who might agree to appear in his book. His main target was the guest of honor, a major Broadway actor.

The writer had to scheme to get access to the event. He knew someone inside the actor's public relations firm, and he used his friendship with her to gain admission to the party.

As luck would have it, he couldn't get near the guest of honor. But he spoke to several people who had some connection to the actor. He eventually "networked" with an attorney who was a partner of the actor's attorney. From there the writer was able to obtain an interview with the actor himself.

Whether you are trying to attract the support of the rich and powerful or just your boss, remember that everyone knows someone. If you can't approach your target directly, get to know those who influence this person. They may not be powerful themselves, and probably aren't famous or rich—but they are more accessible. Of course, a contact doesn't always lead to a connection with a powerful person, but it can be an important first step.

Be Accessible

You must do more than network. You must allow others to reach you. In other words, you must be accessible to those whose support you desire. Achieving accessibility is part science, part art. It means establishing a presence even when you are not there physically.

Accessibility means being reachable at home, in the car, or on the job. In one sense this is as much a technological problem as anything else. There are a variety of means of increasing accessibility, including installing an answering machine, carrying a pager, or getting a car phone. At work it can mean working overtime to help a superior finish a project, or skipping lunch to discuss a problem with a peer or co-worker.

Show a Desire for Support

If you want the support of friends, family, lovers, and colleagues, you must make known what your needs are. We often assume erroneously that others automatically know our needs for emotional support, sponsorship, or image building and have decided they cannot or will not meet those needs. In fact, others may be totally unaware of the nature and extent of our needs.

Pursue Support Aggressively

Take the initiative when seeking support. Many of my respondents basically live by this maxim in order to accomplish their goals.

Carl, age 40, had spent most of his career in academia. A Ph.D. in psychology, he had been denied tenure at age 35. He realized that he would have to seek employment outside of the university setting. He hadn't the vaguest idea of how to make the transition into the "real world."

He sought the help of a trusted advisor, a former professor, who steered him toward management consulting. Once Carl had made the decision to enter the world of the independent entrepreneur, he pursued support aggressively. He contacted every ex-colleague whose phone number he had, picking their brains on the fine points of setting up a consulting firm, locating clients, and selling the product.

It took Carl three years, but he made a successful transition. He had to learn everything from scratch, from financing to business etiquette, and he required loans, office help, and contacts. He let others know that he needed help, while simultaneously inquiring how he could meet their needs.

The lesson is clear: If you want to build a supporting cast, your days as a recluse must end. You must get out there and connect.

As you can see, support is a complicated phenomenon, and there are many different reasons why people support others. Just think of why you may feel compelled to help people you encounter: some seem charismatic, some are just plain likable, others seem like winners whom you may want to enlist in your supporting cast because they can help you achieve your goals.

This chapter should have helped you to assess your own ability to draw support, as well as to understand what attracts you to others. Of course, your ability to attract others is affected by a multitude of factors, the beginnings of which are often rooted in your earlier life. Parents, teachers, and childhood friends have all helped shape your current personality. In the next chapter we will explore your past experiences to understand their effect on you and your ability to attract a supporting cast.

CHAPTER FOUR

Looking Back—Your Support Up to Now

The ability to succeed—and to feel comfortable with success—starts early in life. Childhood experiences with parents, teachers, and others exert a profound influence on later life status.

In this chapter we will examine those early participants in your life—parents, teachers, relatives, and peers—to better understand what kind of supports you had growing up, and what might have been missing in your early childhood networks:

- What levels of support have you experienced up to this point in your life?

- Who were your biggest supporters during your early life?

- Were there people in your background who held you back?

- How have past relationships with parents, teachers, and guardians affected your current level of success?

75

- Early on, did you have the advisors, cheerleaders, and role models so critical to success?

Most successful people with whom I have spoken seem to have a firm grasp on their past—they understand just what contributions key individuals made to their characters and their lives. By the time you finish reading this chapter, you too will have a pretty good idea of the contribution your early support system has made to your life and your ability to succeed.

WHY EARLY SUPPORTERS ARE SO IMPORTANT

Those winning attributes discussed in the last chapter, such as self-confidence, adaptability, competence, even energy level, are all developed through early experiences with others. Here are just some of the areas of your adult life that are shaped by your early supporters.

Sense of Self-worth

Your sense of self, what you think of your abilities, competence, and your feeling of attractiveness, is deeply rooted in early experiences with parents, teachers, and peers.

Ability to Perform

Your upbringing affects your competence in many ways. If your parents instilled in you a strong self-image, you will approach your job and career with confidence in your performance ability. The more highly you think of yourself, the greater your ability to do your job properly. You will also be more likely to take the risks necessary to get ahead. The knowledge, advice, and financial assistance you received as a youngster should also help you in the long run to become a better performer in life.

Propensity to Give

Your ability to succeed is directly related to your willingness to help others reach their own goals. But many of us can give only if we ourselves have been the recipients of love, affection, and attention. The person who has benefited from others' generosity is more likely now to extend that support to others. On the other hand, an adult whose childhood was emotionally impoverished has no storehouse of generosity from which to draw when others request support.

It takes a secure person to be really giving. If you are still trying to gain the ego gratification and attention that you were denied as a child, you will have difficulty meeting another's needs.

Compensating for Deficits

What if, after reading this chapter, you realize that your parents, teachers, and peers did not provide the supports they should have? Where does this new knowledge leave you? The answer is quite simple: you will have to go out and compensate for these deficits. If you had poor advisors, no catalysts, no image builders or cheerleaders early in life, then you must begin to seek them now. We will be spending the better part of this book exploring ways for you to expand and develop your supporting cast.

Of all those who played a role in your development, your "significant others"—most notably your parents—probably had the most profound influence on you. Did they do all they could to turn you into a high achiever?

DID YOUR PARENTS BUILD YOUR SELF-ESTEEM?

Self-image is not something we can create out of sheer will-power. It is built by parents and others with whom we interact and whose opinion we respect.

If as children we are told we are beautiful, worthy of success, and competent, we will most likely act in accordance with those images throughout our lives. But if we are bombarded with negative images of ourselves, we may spend the rest of our lives either living within the constraints of these images, or fighting an uphill battle to convince ourselves that these negative images are untrue.

Did your parents provide the kinds of supports that lay the foundation for success?

Did They Give You Attention?

Children equate their parents' attention with approval. The parents' generosity with attention greatly affects the development of the child's self-image. To meet your needs in this area, your parents should have been accessible to you during critical times and key experiences, such as when you performed, received awards, or competed in sports.

One of my respondents remembers how her parents went out of their way to see her dance in many school performances. Just knowing that they were watching, she says, made her feel special.

Were your parents there for you at critical moments in your life? Did they show excitement at your accomplishments? Psychologist Erik Erikson claims that children need this type of feedback in order to develop what he calls a sense of "industry." Children feel wanted and special when they produce something of value. According to Erikson, these early celebrations of accomplishments serve as rewards that encourage the child to continue to achieve throughout life.

One of the more successful executives I interviewed re-counts that even when he brought home amateurish works of art, his mother offered praise. Many parents think it dishon-est to praise a child's less-than-important accomplishments. Not so. The child may perceive any lack of enthusiasm as disapproval.

Another successful executive claims that his parents built his self-confidence by having him recount to them something good that happened to him in school each day. In effect they taught him to identify and enjoy good experiences and in the process helped him to condition himself to want to replicate those positive feelings. By playing the celebrator role to the fullest, they were encouraging him to focus on his ability to achieve.

Parental enthusiasm about children's accomplishments helps to instill in children an image of themselves as success-prone individuals. In Erikson's view, if we don't receive this early encouragement, we end up believing that somehow we let our parents down. We may even develop a sense of guilt over what we perceive as our inability to measure up to our parents' expectations.

Much of the ability to achieve is based on self-confidence. Many people become successful because they have the confi-dence to make speeches, dictate rules, and give opinions as if the whole world hung on their every word. This only comes about because their parents took them seriously early on. The child who is used to getting attention comes to expect and demand attention later in life.

To a large extent these people prove the theory that we get what we expect. High achievers don't get others to support their quest for success just by asking for support. By their very actions, they literally demand it! People who are on the receiv-ing end of such demands reason that if someone has the nerve to demand attention, they must deserve it. The requests create their own legitimacy.

Obviously, the more seriously your parents and significant

others took you, the more self-confidence you bring to each career and life situation. The less support you had in this area in childhood, the more you must concentrate on recruiting celebrators into your current supporting cast. You should use your awareness of the deficiencies in your past to help you become more successful in the future.

Did They Give You Compliments?

Were your parents generous with compliments? Many parents don't realize how important it is to bestow accolades on a child for good work. The more specific and sincere the compliments, the more effective they are as esteem builders.

Why is praise, especially from parents, such an important determinant of later success?

- The more you are complimented as a child, the more you will learn to expect recognition for your accomplishments as an adult.

- You probably won't develop the annoying tendency as an adult to demand approval from others for the slightest good act to compensate for the praise you didn't receive as a child.

- Since you have come to expect compliments, you accept them graciously when they do come your way.

- If you were complimented early, you know how good it feels to receive praise. You will be more proficient at using praise as a way to attract others and to convince them to join your supporting cast.

You must examine closely how a lack of compliments and general rewards for jobs well done has affected your current ability to build a supporting cast. Perhaps you should be recruiting more cheerleaders to make up for early deficiencies.

WERE YOUR PARENTS GOOD ADVISORS?

One of the most crucial support roles that parents play is that of advisor. If, as you matured, your parents showed you how the world operated, today you should be in a good position to deal with many of life's demands. Let's look at some of the more valuable lessons about life and success that your parents should have taught you.

Did They Teach You How the World Works?

To be truly successful, you must be able to understand how the world works: what motivates others, how one event connects with another, the processes and rationales underlying the actions and movements of people and things.

Did your parents attempt to make sense of the world to you? Did they explain why people acted the way they did, how events unfolded? Many successful managers and executives claim that their parents were more than willing to play this role in their lives.

For example, in his autobiography, Chrysler Corporation chairman Lee Iacocca emphasizes how his father helped teach him how the world works. His father told him that problems are inevitable in any project or business, that all life has its ups and downs, and that disappointments are part of everyone's life. Iacocca claims that because of his father's explanation of the ebb and flow of life, he was never discouraged by setbacks. They weren't necessarily a sign of personal failings, but just part of the process.

Your parents served you well if they taught you how the world works. Unfortunately, some parents easily tire of their children's endless questions, and some are downright intimidated by the more technical scientific questions emerging from their offspring's imagination. To become a high achiever, you need to examine your relationship with your parents to determine to what extent they played this advisory role in your life.

Did They Open Up the World of Careers?

Did your family discuss careers? Did they talk about the opportunities in a variety of occupations, and in general direct you to the fields that would give you the greatest opportunity for achieving success?

Some parents, while supportive in other areas, have a hard time moving their children in the right career direction. They may have limited knowledge of various occupations, and little idea of which fields will be in strongest demand and which may become obsolete.

But even if your parents could not give you specific advice on occupations, they may have offered you valuable encouragement to become successful. Supportive parents are those who, regardless of their understanding of the occupational sphere, encourage their children to "be someone," to follow their dreams. Nonsupportive parents just let their children drift.

Regardless of the field you wanted to enter, your parents played the advisor role well if they helped you to envision success and encouraged you to achieve certain goals. If you are hesitant as an adult to follow your dreams, you may only have to remember your parents' warnings of danger to understand the cause of your present insecurities. You need to recruit into your supporting cast advisors and cheerleaders to compensate for these early shortcomings.

DID YOUR PARENTS HELP YOU BECOME INDEPENDENT?

In a recent *Fortune* magazine article, Bob Allen, chairman of AT&T, attributes his success to the fact that his parents encouraged him to acquire a sense of responsibility early. He has held jobs since he was eight years old—delivering newspapers, cutting grass, working on a pipeline, and then a railroad gang. His parents knew that these jobs would give him the sense of independence that would help make him a success later on.

A similar ethic operated during childhood for Morris and Michael Kaplan, whose family business, the Kaplan organization, is a major real estate development corporation. The children of refugees from Nazi Germany, the Kaplans were taught early to "sink or swim" as workers in their father's business. Michael, the eldest son, reports in an article in *New Jersey Success,* "Ours is not a hand-holding business." If they wanted to participate, the senior Kaplan informed them, they had to learn the business from the bottom up. And they did. They both slowly became part of the organization by performing various jobs around the building sites—shoveling snow, working as ordinary laborers.

The lesson is clear. While developing a strong sense of self-worth and acquiring knowledge of the world were important, your chances of becoming successful were greatly enhanced if your parents taught you how to live and act independently. In fact, the greatest favor your parents could have done for you was to help you develop a sense that you could meet any challenge, overcome any difficulties of adult life.

Your parents may have tried different approaches to instill in you a sense of independence. They may have had you perform extra chores around the house. As a child you may have resented this work, but the tasks served to develop your faith in your abilities. As one manager says:

> I turned out better than 90 percent of the kids today. Everything I have I worked for, because my mother taught me to be independent. My friends don't know how to work hard, and are more "consuming" than "producing."

Some parents believe that encouraging a child to participate in sports helps to develop a sense of independence. One mother puts it this way:

Sports helps children develop independence because it
helps them feel confident in the bodily sense. If the child
is good at swimming or tennis, his ability to thrive in this
respect helps him believe he can do well on his own.

Regardless of how parents choose to teach responsibility,
the truly supportive ones do so without robbing their children
of childhood and adolescence. While they help their offspring
achieve independence through hard work and discipline, they
also give them a certain amount of free time to invent their
own personalities, to dream. They realize that this creative
side must be allowed free rein. They want to create a balance
between a sense of responsibility through hard work and a
sense of playfulness and creativity through leisure.

The noted psychologist Jean Piaget pointed out that play
and leisure serve a major role in children's cognitive and
moral development. In games, children learn to play within
the rules and to create their own universe, both necessary
skills if one is to achieve a measure of independence in the
adult world.

Of course, some of us travel a less gentle road to independence. One successful young entrepreneur learned independence under particularly rough circumstances. His father had
walked out on the family when the boy was barely in his
teens. His mother worked, and for the most part he was left to
his own devices. At age 13 he was already working, and never
stopped working through college. "I think being on my own
early, not being able to depend on others, allowed me to
develop an independent thought pattern," he says.

Remember, developing an air of independence has an important side benefit: it will attract others into your supporting
cast. The more independent (and the less needy) you appear,
the more willing people will be to offer their support. And the
more supporters you have, the more successful you will
become.

Financial Independence

A primary supporting cast role your parents played was that of financier. They put food on the table, paid your doctor bills, perhaps financed your education.

In addition to this direct assistance, your parents may have helped you financially in an even more important way. By preparing you for the day when you would leave home and could no longer rely on them for direct financial assistance, they may have established the groundwork for your later financial independence.

Most parents want to give their children all the information they will need in order to achieve financial security. But they rarely have a clue how to go about doing this. Their ill-trained offspring travel a predictable path to financial chaos. They have no idea how to plan a budget or balance a checkbook. When audited, they scurry around for days looking for receipts. Always in debt, they are happy if they can meet the mortgage and the interest payments on their Mastercard. Because they are not in control of their financial situation, they can never become truly independent.

Did your parents help you become financially independent by being good models of sound financial behavior and directly demonstrating money-saving techniques? For instance, did they:

- Give you an allowance and show you how to budget it?
- Give you some freedom in spending this allowance?
- Include you in family discussions regarding spending and budget?
- Allow you to participate in family shopping?

Educators say that these early learning experiences are directly related to later ability to become financially responsible and secure. If you have a hard time getting your financial house in order, you should begin recruiting financiers into your supporting cast. Such people are not necessarily those who lend you money; they may be accountants and consultants who can show you how to manage your monetary affairs yourself.

DID YOUR PARENTS ENCOURAGE YOU TO BECOME AMBITIOUS?

Like self-esteem and independence, ambition is a trait that can be fostered by early strong parental support. Without such support, it is difficult for a person to develop this drive.

Many of the successful executives I interviewed credit at least one parent with inculcating in them the drive to succeed. One particular executive was one of five children, and although his father was rarely around, his mother, grandmother, and aunt were always there to motivate him to succeed. "I was always encouraged to go to college, and was encouraged to continue to work, even as a night auditor," he recalls. There were times when he was tempted to drop out of school, but his family convinced him to stick with it in spite of the hardships. Those lessons in ambition stayed with him for the rest of this life.

Did your parents provide you with the drive to succeed? You may be wondering how anyone can do this for a child—through pep talks, admonishments, threats? Let's look at how parents of successful individuals help instill ambition in their children.

They make the concept of success real and attainable. They may serve as a role model for the child, using their own lives as proof that success is possible. Successful people may be regular guests in their home. Thus their kids realize that success isn't just for "other people," that success is normal and should happen to them as well.

They encourage the child to "think big." The child is allowed to enjoy the fantasy of becoming president of a company, a great inventor, a media star, a famous person. The less the parents censor the child's more ambitious fantasies—the more they allow her to imagine herself as a superior achiever—the greater the chance that she will be able to envision, and hence create, her own success.

They let the child enjoy some of the fruits of the good life. Upper-middle-class parents understand this well. While they don't want to spoil their child, they want him to learn that hard work and perseverance have definite rewards. They let the child enjoy vacations, make reasonable purchases, and enjoy the lifestyle that his parents have constructed out of their own hard work and talent.

They expose the child to biographies of successful people, especially those who could be described as "self-made." The parents thus teach the child to respect the achievements of others and to understand that any accomplishment requires determination and hard work.

They choose schools carefully. Aware of the influence of peers on later success, many parents try to stack the deck in favor of their children by choosing the best schools. They hope that attending the "right" school will encourage the child to be ambitious. The right school will also provide the child with a pool of friends and schoolmates who may share what the parents consider the proper attitude toward success and achievement.

Did your parents encourage your ambitions, or did they present you with a thousand "no's," reasons why you couldn't or shouldn't achieve your loftier goals? In the latter case, you should consider recruiting esteem builders and catalysts into your supporting cast.

Donald Trump's autobiography *The Art of the Deal* suggests that Trump's father fulfilled many of the preceding roles for his son. A real estate developer during the 1930s and 1940s, Trump's father served as a combination role model and teacher. He was generous when it came to exposing his son to the intricacies of the real estate business. Most important, the father developed in the son a sense of ambition and independence. The younger Trump learned that he could accomplish anything if he was willing to pay the price of perseverance and hard work.

WHEN PARENTS TRY TO GET THE COMPETITIVE EDGE

If your parents did not support you in many of the ways we have just described, it could have been simply because they did not understand your needs. However, there is sometimes a more discomforting reason for low parental support. Some parents withdraw support, or never really offer it, because they feel threatened by their children. A few parents secretly resent the accomplishments, talent, or good looks of one of their children. Often a parent, while perfectly willing to help and support a mediocre son or daughter, may inadvertently begin to envy a more talented child. The reasons for this are many: insecurities, frustrations over missed chances in the parent's own life, or even out-and-out maliciousness.

In some cases parents inadvertently enter into competition with their child, to the detriment of the child's well-being. Because they see the child as a threat, parents do not compliment him when he does well, deny him opportunities to prove himself, and may in fact overtly denigrate his achievements.

Did your parents compete with you? As a child, you probably didn't have the slightest inkling that your parent might be obstructing your path to success out of jealousy. Often it's not until their twenties that people discover that envy was at the root of some of the parental disapproval they suffered. By that time, the damage is done. They have internalized two decades of slights or denigrating remarks, and now they carry the weight of self-doubt and feelings of inferiority.

Unless you attempt to undo the damage done to you by a competitive parent, you will never really believe that you are competent, talented, and worthy of success. You will have internalized the belief that you really don't have the capability to achieve your goals.

If this has been your experience, the best solution is either to work out the results of the destructive relationship in therapy or other formal structured environments or to weave your mate and friends into a strong supporting cast. Such a support system can do much to undo the damage. It can often become a parental substitute, creating ego builders that you should have had much earlier in life. Your support group can provide the emotional foundation from which you can launch your career and life.

In a good supporting cast, as in a healthy parental relationship, criticism is laced with caring, not envy; advice is meant to help, not hurt; and your every gain is perceived as your own achievement, not someone else's loss.

If you don't have a strong supporting cast to "re-parent" you, build one now!

THE ENVIRONMENT AT LARGE

Although parents probably have the greatest influence on our early development, peers, teachers, and siblings contribute greatly to this process. They also can affect our self-esteem, self-confidence, and level of ambition.

What Did You Really Learn in School?

From many students' points of view, the status of teachers as bearers of authority and knowledge imbues them with a credibility that makes their word almost godlike. Thus it is important to students that their teachers like and respect them. I'm sure you remember the warm feelings you experienced when a favorite teacher complimented you, encouraged you, or took a strong interest in your development. Conversely, if your teachers had a poor opinion of you, chances are you picked up these negative signals.

Although expected to be objective about their students and fair in their evaluations of them, teachers are as prone to prejudice and bias as anyone else. They may have based their opinion of you not so much on your abilities as your looks, your parents, your sex, your socioeconomic background, or the companions they observed you eating with in the school cafeteria.

If you were unfortunate enough to experience teacher bias, did your teachers' low opinions about your abilities make you begin to doubt your self-worth? Many of the less successful respondents in my research were victims of poor teacher support in high school. But lack of support from teachers does not doom you to failure. Parental support is more important.

Some people labeled deficient by teachers and guidance counselors succeed in spite of this. One person, challenged by his teachers' conception of him as a low-potential student, sought every opportunity to prove them wrong. You may be surprised to learn that Albert Einstein was considered a relatively mediocre student by his teachers. It is rumored that he even received failing grades in math. For years he was considered a poor candidate for university teaching, which explains why he was working at a patent office at the time he published the papers on relativity that made him famous.

Sometimes schools just let students languish. One successful publisher attended a very competitive high school and received average grades. His undistinguished record continued through college, until he realized that he was in the wrong field. He changed majors, became an honor student, and addressed his school's commencement exercises.

Happily, many executives I spoke to describe a school environment that loaded the dice in their favor. In some schools, it seems, students can't help but turn out successful. The environment is such that everybody is expected to graduate, to go on to a good college, and to become "rich and famous," or something like it.

One executive claims that at the high school he attended, even children from poor families began to believe they could achieve anything they wanted to.

> I don't think I could have failed if I had wanted to, primarily because in the network I was growing up in, teachers made me be successful. If I turned in a poor homework assignment, I was quickly told that I must do better. If I was falling behind the others, the teachers were quick to let me know it.

Some schools have established an environment of excellence where failure is not considered an option. Some schools implant early in the child the expectation that he or she can achieve greatness.

Jacqueline Kennedy Onassis was determined that her children, John and Caroline, should not go to the "society" schools that she had attended. She wanted to prepare them for careers, not a lifetime of the enjoyment of riches. She placed them in academically tough schools where they would be intellectually challenged and would have standards of excellence instilled in them.

Did your teachers have a high regard for your ability? Did they encourage you to succeed? Did they take the time to impart their knowledge to you? Did they train you properly?

If the answer to these questions is yes, your teachers and school in general were good members of your supporting cast. But if you feel you were shortchanged in the support area, you're not alone. Many people have experienced the same neglect. They have learned to overcome this deficit by developing a strong supporting cast, by recruiting the esteem builders, advisors, and sponsors that their early schooling did not provide.

Peer Support

Looking back, do you feel that your early peers delivered everything you would want from cast members today? Did they serve as cheerleaders, contacts, catalysts, and image builders?

Peers can be as much a determinant of later success as teachers and the school environment. Your ability to achieve can be greatly influenced by whether you fell in with a crowd that just wanted to waste time, or associated with friends who were studious and serious about their future.

Although your peers may have reflected their parents' expectations about success, their standards still influenced your own goals. One woman who grew up in Great Neck, Long Island, where everyone's father was an executive, doctor, or lawyer, described the invisible but potent "community standard" of excellence: "There is no one in Great Neck who doesn't do something important. Just to keep up with them, I went for a Ph.D."

These standards were largely communicated to her by everyday banter and conversations with peers. They discussed dreams and aspirations and, most important, they exchanged strategies on how to achieve these goals. No one comes into this world wanting to go to Harvard and become a doctor. Peers are as important as parents when it comes to forming ideas of the important goals in life.

ARE WOMEN SOCIALIZED DIFFERENTLY?

It is no secret that many women have undergone a different socialization process than males. The differences in socialization patterns between the sexes have been well documented. Men have been directed toward a career, women toward family life. Although parents' treatment of female children is changing, most adult women were not prepared for careers to the same extent as their brothers. Many women find themselves in the position of having to overcome the negative effects of early socialization.

One of my female respondents experienced firsthand the effects of sex-role differentiation. The family expected her brother to become a doctor. They guided him through the early years of his schooling, helping him take (and pass) all the right courses. But his dreams of becoming an M.D. ended when he failed chemistry as an undergrad. Immediately, the parents' career support mechanisms came into play to ensure that he would still become a successful professional. They encouraged him to make whatever curriculum adjustments were necessary to pursue a law career. He is now a successful lawyer, clearing $130,000 per year.

The set of expectations they presented their daughter was quite different, and the supports they supplied her were far short of those provided the brother:

> They always told me I was smart, pretty, but when it came time for me to go to grad school, certainly they didn't encourage me. It was my decision, and it was fine once I made the decision. But they never said "you could be this, or you could be that."

In fact, the best they could come up with in terms of a career for their daughter was the usual grab bag of female professions: teaching, nursing, small-time entrepreneur. Their vision of her career was strictly one that would be ancillary to her husband's profession. "My mother has used the same phrase over and over again: 'You can have a business. Get married, have children, and you can have a little job.'"

Women who were encouraged to pursue their interests have in fact succeeded even in nontraditional areas like science. One successful female engineer was quite clear about the effects of early socialization on her career progress. "I never played with dolls. I was always trying to fix a lawn mower or my parents' air conditioner. I was never discouraged. If I could make things work, great."

But her experience is the exception. Most women find replicated at the corporate level the same mediocre support they experienced during childhood. If you are a woman you probably realize how built-in barriers make it tougher for you than for men to succeed in the worlds of business, science, and academia. Men often still see female managers only as clericals and line supervisors. Subliminally they may even perceive women managers as wives, daughters, and girlfriends. If nothing else, they may see women managers as *temporary*.

Do these perceptions impede a woman's career progress? Ninety-eight percent of senior management in Fortune 500 companies is male, surrounded by clusters of females at the secondary and tertiary management levels. It can be inferred that institutional support for female advancement does not exist in many companies.

Since women often receive neither the early socialization needed for success nor the institutional support for upward mobility, developing a supporting cast is even more important for them. By building a supporting cast, both on the job and off, that can provide the emotional and tactical assistance that may not have been forthcoming in childhood or in job situations, women can overcome deficiencies in early socialization.

UNDERSTANDING YOUR PAST

If after reading this chapter you feel that you have received many of the benefits that supportive parents and others can bestow on a young person, you are probably in good shape. However, this chapter might have revealed to you that certain pieces of your support fabric are missing.

Successercize 3, "Assessing Your Past," should help you analyze the types of support you did or did not receive from parents, teachers, and early friends. Take a few minutes to reflect on your early experiences, and then complete the Successercize.

Assessing Your Past

Think about your early experiences with parents, teachers, and peers, and answer the following questions with regard to these people.

1. Did they instill in you a sense of ambition?   Y   N

2. Do you feel that your parents and others pre-   Y   N
   pared you for financial independence?

3. Do you feel that they did enough to build your   Y   N
   sense of self-esteem?

4. Did your parents and others show excitement   Y   N
   and compliment you when you did well?

5. Did you have enough leisure time in child-   Y   N
   hood to express the creative side of yourself,
   to play, to invent?

6. Were there always people around with whom   Y   N
   you could talk through your problems?

7. Were you surrounded by a number of suc-   Y   N
   cessful role models whom you could later
   emulate?

8. Did your parents and others provide you with   Y   N
   information on careers and occupations that
   you later found useful?

9. Do you feel that your parents and teachers   Y   N
   evaluated your actions fairly?

10. Did they offer you constructive criticism when   Y   N
it was needed?

If you answered many of these questions "no," then you were lacking the early supports that many successful people report receiving. But don't become discouraged. Use this knowledge as the first step in your search for people who can fulfill the roles that parents and others did not.

This chapter should have helped you confront the variety of early influences that either helped or hindered your ability to achieve your goals today. If early supports were lacking, you must work to overcome negative self-images by surrounding yourself with people who support a more desirable self-concept, and filter out those who do not. Don't do as so many others have and literally duplicate in adult life the nonsupport patterns of childhood.

The rest of this book will help you to build on the support roles your early influences did provide and to develop strategies for compensating for those roles not fulfilled early on.

In the preceding chapter we began to examine ways in which you can attract people in general. Next we will explore the ways in which you can garner support—on the job, in daily life, and from your mate or lover.

CHAPTER FIVE

Building a Supporting Cast Where You Work

Most of us work. About 95 percent of adult men and 54 percent of adult women are in the labor force. Work seems to be our major preoccupation regardless of our other responsibilities. Even the majority of mothers of toddlers work full time. And those not yet working are preparing to enter the work force—whether in high schools, universities, training programs, apprenticeships, or internships.

We spend the better part of our waking moments pursuing our occupation. What time we have away from the workplace we spend traveling to and from our jobs, and it seems that everyone brings work home these days. It can be said that for many, their job is their life. Career and career success have become a national obsession.

What are your career goals? Do you want to build a career with your current employer? Do you want to build a sufficient number of contacts, experience, and résumé points so that you can leave your company for another? Or do you see your work for an organization to be a transitional phase en route to one in which you are your own boss, the owner of your own business?

Regardless of your long-term career goals, you need to develop a supporting cast to achieve success. If you want to progress at your present company, you will have to develop a cast filled with sponsors and advisors from above and constructive critics from below.

Even if you wish to use your job as a stepping-stone, you will need to prove yourself to the people there. You may need them as contacts and public relations specialists to help you locate jobs elsewhere.

In this chapter we will examine how you can develop the supporting cast you need for high achievement in your career. As you will see, developing alliances among peers, subordinates, and superiors is a critical factor in job success.

WHO REALLY GETS SUPPORT IN AN ORGANIZATION?

Most of this chapter will be concerned with how to spot potential supporters in your organization and how to go about attracting their attention and garnering their support. Before we discuss the "how to" of building a supporting cast, let's look briefly at the traits that business respondents mention as the ones they find particularly attractive in employees:

- Commitment to the organization
- A demonstrated sense of responsibility
- Competence
- A willingness to take risks
- Trustworthiness
- An ability to maintain confidences
- Intelligence
- Organizational savvy

These are only some of the traits you should consider developing to attract the support of higher-ups. Keep in mind that the way you dress, your technical skills, and the trust you inspire will also enter into the total image that will attract potential supporters.

This image is in part built upon your reputation—what people in the organization think of your abilities. This is why having credible supporters in the organization will help you expand your power base. If some members of your supporting cast play the public relations role for you, you will be in an excellent position to draw others into your supporting cast.

What If You Are a Newcomer?

If you are new to an organization, of course, you have no reputation upon which to build, no known strong points to exploit. However, your neophyte status may actually be considered an attractive quality by many higher-ups.

For one thing, veterans like to help people who they perceive as "wet behind the ears." Some people get a feeling of power by helping others less savvy than themselves. Second, people in power are seldom inclined to see a new lower-level employee as a threat. Their power and authority are so much greater than the entry-level person's that they cannot conceive of the newcomer in any way threatening their position and security. Plus, as one respondent says, organizations put a premium on "new blood"—employees who will revitalize the corporation with their energy and enthusiasm.

So when you first enter an organization, try to exploit the glow that surrounds your new status as much as possible while it lasts. This is a propitious time to make alliances. In the early stages, while you are still a neophyte, you should try to catch the ear and eye of someone higher up the hierarchy.

HOW TO SPOT THE POWERFUL PEOPLE
IN AN ORGANIZATION

Before you begin to attract others, you must know who in the carcompany can truly support you in your goals. In short, you must be able to identify your company's key players.

Above all, look for people who have outstanding careers. They may be those who have risen rapidly in the company, are young for their position, and are well regarded by others. Their contributions to the company's direction, policies, technologies, and overall development make them organizational winners. These are the people who will shape the company's future, who have the organizational power and influence to give you the support you need to move ahead.

Your problem, of course, is to locate such people. To do so, you must develop an understanding of the subtleties of your company's power structure. Most organizations really have two power structures: a formal one and an informal one. It is sometimes difficult, especially for a neophyte, to realize that a powerful-sounding title and official position do not necessarily confer real power. In the political arena, for instance, a president's unofficial advisor may have more influence over national decisions than the secretary of defense.

You must become familiar with both the formal and informal power structures if you are to identify those people who can help you move ahead.

Your Company's Formal Power Structure

The key to the company's formal power structure is its organizational chart. This document will show you which positions are either powerful or connected to other positions of authority. For instance, one of my respondents is vice president of operations for the patient-care division of a huge pharmaceutical conglomerate. He reports to a president of the company, who reports to a group president, who in turn reports to the CEO. By studying his position on the organizational chart, you would realize that by attracting his support you may have a connection to the top of the organization, since he occasionally rubs elbows with the CEO.

The organizational chart may also reveal which divisions within an organization are the most important. Many companies keep their organizational or divisional charts in booklets, with one division's page laid on top of another, so that you can in essence "read" the organizational structure, front to back. As one manager told me:

> The divisions follow one another, page by page, the most important coming before the next most important, all following the "president's page." In our company, the product development function is the most important. This division's "page" in the organizational chart follows the president's page.

When a company's organizational structure is accessible in this way, it is easy for you to discern where the most powerful people are located.

You can also look at the title of the head of a particular division to determine how important that division is. It may be "group vice president," or "vice president," or just plain old "manager," giving some indication of relative power. Caution: titles mean different things in different companies. A person holding a title like "department chief" or "manager" might have the same function but a more elegant title at another corporation. At AT&T, many department chiefs don't have the staff, budget, and influence they would at another company. So you must investigate how much power actually is vested in a given title before pursuing its owner's support.

The Informal Organization

Title and position aren't everything. If you want to locate powerful supporters, you need to uncover the informal organization and learn how it operates. Here are some guidelines you can use in order to get a better grasp on who is really in a position to help your climb up the corporate ladder.

Who spends time with the higher-ups? One indication of a person's real power is the amount of time he or she spends with those higher up the organizational ladder—the CEO, the divisional manager, or a supervisor.

At one large company, according to one of its managers, "there are only twenty people who you really have to know to get ahead." Who are these twenty? They are the people who encircle the CEO, helping to formulate policy and make decisions. They form the CEO's supporting cast. "If you want to sell a job, an appropriation, if you want to really know what's going on here, it's someone among that twenty that's making it all happen," the manager says.

At Toyota, the people at the "manufacturing representative" level have a great say in ad campaigns, allocations of cars, and the success of the many Toyota franchises. One respondent calls them "the young hotshots." People such as these in any organization could probably help enhance your career.

One indication you should especially look for is who gets a slot on the boss's calendar. The boss's calendar is tight, and only a select few ever get on the schedule. If the boss finds time for someone, it usually indicates that this person is either already powerful or is on the way to becoming a power broker in the organization.

In most organizations, the people a step or two removed from higher-ups may be approachable and particularly valuable to you as supporters. Try to find someone close enough to your daily activity so that you can make an impression and develop a close working relationship.

Who gets his or her ideas embraced? An organization always has creative options in terms of policy and product direction. But usually only a few people have sufficient credibility to convince the top person that their ideas are best. Who are these creative or powerful individuals?

If there are three or four directions in which your company can go, and several key players are delivering suggestions, look closely at whose ideas are ultimately embraced by the top executive. This will tell you who is on the way up. As one senior manager suggests:

> Does the ultimate force adopt the ideas of one individual over another, or over a couple of others? That process, over a period of time, helps you begin to understand who has the top person's ear, mind, and attention.

Use meetings to identify the company winners. Meetings provide even the most inexperienced participant with insights into the subtle dynamics that make up the real power structure. Who does the boss turn to for support, backup, or particular expertise?

For instance, if John serves up a suggestion and the executive running the meeting looks at Ellen and asks, "What do you think of that?" Ellen has considerable influence in the organization. If you doubt that others perceive this extra attention as an indication of power, just watch how friendly lower-level people will be to someone like Ellen after the meeting.

You'll hear it through the grapevine. The better your connection to sources of information, the better position you will be in to understand the power structure. If you want to judge someone's real power in the organization, listen to what the grapevine has to say about this person. When approached in informal settings, co-workers are often willing to discuss their opinions on who is where in the company's pecking order.

The office as a power indicator. If you want to determine who is powerful in an organization, analyze the relative location and size of offices. For example, the person with the office closest to the president's is likely to be one of the more influential people in the organization. Anyone the president sees on a daily basis begins to establish a top-of-mind awareness with the key player, and also may be able to circumvent formal channels in getting some valuable time with the company chief.

Organizations really do rank people by their office size, location, and accoutrements. At AT&T, for instance, lower-level managers have cubicles or work stations. The more powerful the manager, the higher the walls around his cubicle. At the upper levels of the corporate hierarchy, managers get actual offices. A window is the final seal of approval.

These are more than status symbols. They indicate how much real power a person has. Become aware of your company's office hierarchy. Who gets leather furniture, and who Naugahyde? Who gets original art and jade sculptures, who gets posters? Who gets plush carpeting, who gets vinyl tiles?

Who is given power and responsibility? The projects and tasks that an individual is assigned are another indicator of his or her power. Who does the crucial project work, and who does the number crunching? Even at the high levels there are projects that are creative, high-visibility endeavors and others that are routine. Take a close look at the people who are asked to head various task forces and strategy teams.

The more you are tuned into the grapevine, the better the chances that you will learn of the assignment of projects to key individuals. You will also have a better insight into what projects are critical to the overall direction and future of the organization.

Who is friends with whom? When trying to identify who is powerful and who is not, keep your eye on the informal relationships and friendships that develop in the organization. Who eats lunch with whom, who socializes with whom, who seem to be having discussions together are all indicators of linkages between people. Social events such as office parties and picnics also serve as reliable indicators of who congregates around the central power.

Staying Power Is Real Power

Often in today's corporate climate, only the more powerful survive. Many a company is undergoing an often brutal downsizing, retaining only the people who matter most to the organization's future and trimming whomever they consider to be part of the company's "fat."

People who have survived several staff reductions are usually among the most powerful people in the organization. They have demonstrated endurance and can most likely teach you the necessary survival skills. In addition, they are probably connected to the power bases in the organization and should be in a good position to give you the career supports that you need.

FINDING THE BEST SUPPORTERS

Organizational clout is one of the more basic ways that a higher-up can qualify as a member of your supporting cast. But does this mean that because a person holds organizational power, you should automatically try to recruit him or her as a potential supporter? The answer is no. Power alone is not sufficient to qualify someone as a good corporate supporter.

You must also consider the amount of career, organizational, and technical information people possess, and how willing they are to share what they know. Competence is also a factor. You don't want a poor performer, regardless of how high up that person is in the power structure. Use the grapevine to assess how the organization judges the potential support member's talent and ability.

You should also try to ascertain whether this person is emotionally secure enough to be able to handle your future success maturely. If you surpass this person, will he or she resent you enough to withdraw support or otherwise sabotage your career? To answer such questions, you might want to inquire into the extent to which the person in question supports others or has been supported by others.

Lastly, many people seriously consider only those supporters with whom they can establish good "chemistry." They want to be sure that their personal styles mesh. Some people want supporters with whom they can feel comfortable and joke around.

Keep in mind, however, that the amount of chemistry needed between you and an office support member is partly a function of what role this person will play. If the only role you want a powerful individual to play is that of sponsor, then the chemistry issue may not be significant. But if you want a supporter with whom you can discuss your private life in confidence, you should not choose someone who sees organizational relationships as pure business. In this case, the perfect boss-level supporter is one who doesn't mind sharing some of his personal life with you and who doesn't feel uncomfortable when you talk about personal issues, such as conflicts between your home life and the job.

In other words, if you want your organizational supporting cast to serve as cheerleaders, celebrators, constructive critics, as well as job sponsors, personality mesh may be an important consideration when choosing the perfect supporter.

HOW TO ATTRACT SUPPORT FROM ABOVE

In this section we will deal with the art of gaining visibility. You've targeted potential supporters; now you will work on making the contact and establishing the relationship.

Many of us feel that the way to gain visibility is merely to do our job well. Unfortunately, we must be more than competent—we must be noticed! One senior manager puts it this way:

> I know some very talented people who have not progressed as far as I have in the organization, and in fact have lagged behind others with less talent. Their problem is that no one knows how talented they really are.

According to one executive, you must really work at bursting out of the scene.

> Even in the most mundane kind of task, I have always tried to make sure that there was some kind of flair, some kind of spin, that made that job kind of special. So that might have drawn attention to myself.

You must learn to create avenues of visibility, to exploit opportunities to be recognized for the results you produce. Let's look at some of the ways that top business people have been able to gain the visibility needed to attract supporters.

Be accessible. As Woody Allen once said, "Seventy percent of success is just showing up." While he may have overestimated the percentage, there is no doubt that you will enhance your visibility and attract supporters by being around when certain things are happening.

Accessibility means having people in the organization know how to find you. Do you always leave a message with co-workers and secretaries as to your whereabouts? Are you usually aware of the developments in your company, so that you can be at the right place at the right time? Do higher-ups know where to find you in an emergency?

Accessibility is more than being available. It is an attitude. Some people by their very demeanor make it understood that they would rather not be involved in any work-related activity that's "not their job." If you want to earn support, you must make it known that you are available to extend your contribution to the organization beyond your job description.

Take risks. Achieving visibility sometimes contains an element of risk. Not all of us want to take calculated risks to get ahead, and in fact may wish that we could avoid taking any risks. But according to one senior executive, in today's business environment you will not get any support if you appear to be "standing still" or risk-averse.

> Ten or fifteen years ago, you could probably get by without taking any risks. But in this era of competition and productivity, you are living in a risk environment just to get your product rolling along. There has been an across-the-board policy of higher competition.

The managers who were instrumental in reviving Chrysler in the early 1980s all reaped career benefits from their actions. Similar rewards accrued to the key players in Johnson & Johnson's reaction to the 1982 Tylenol product-tampering case. Not only did they successfully navigate the company through choppy political waters, but they did it visibly.

Many of the people who essentially put their necks on the

line in order to save these companies were later rewarded with the support of the top executives, who were glad to be identified as sponsors and supporters of those people who had just saved their company. Many of critical players in the rescue operation later became group presidents, part of that immediate ring around the CEO.

In many corporations today, you need to put yourself on the line. If successful, you will have no dearth of supporters. Fail, and you will be looking for another job.

You must determine how much risk you are willing to take in attracting a supporting cast. The more risk, the greater the chance that you will gain supporters.

Serve on projects. Serve on as many key projects as possible to gain the visibility necessary to attract support—but take care that these projects have a good chance of succeeding. If your projects get off the ground, you will indeed become an attractive candidate for a higher position.

If necessary, volunteer for assignments, especially those that afford you the opportunity to rub shoulders with corporate movers and shakers. They will become familiar with your talent and get to know you on a more equal, informal basis.

Initiate projects. Another mode of gaining visibility is to initiate a project on your own. One middle manager describes this method of getting the eye of senior management:

> Pretty soon I will propose several million dollars in appropriations to start a new project. If I am successful in launching this venture, it will be impossible for them to not know that I am the one behind it.

The project could be anything from initiating a task force to study a new market, to establishing a new product. The important thing is that you exhibit both creativity and a propensity to take risks.

Once you have initiated the project, you must be certain to assume a decision-making role. Merely serving in the endeavor, no matter how competently, could imply to possible supporters that you are not a main driver. People are more attracted to taskmasters than task doers.

Ask questions of superiors. A key method of gaining support from superiors is to ask questions or request information from them. Why, you may wonder, would a senior executive be attracted to someone who for all practical purposes is putting himself in the student role?

For one thing, seniors like giving advice, especially if it is followed. There is a bit of altruism in all of us. But, more important, by asking advice you are in effect telling higher-ups that their knowledge, wisdom, and information are valuable. You might be according credibility to their worldview or philosophy as few colleagues or superiors have done. In effect, you may be making your superiors feel important, credible, and authoritative.

Take on others' work. Offer assistance to someone more senior. When you volunteer to help, you are giving out a signal that you are interested in transcending your job description. Because you are seen as having a broader perspective, you achieve top-of-mind awareness as a person to whom the senior executive can turn when people are needed for key projects and task forces.

This extra effort tells higher-ups that you are flexible and want to expand your responsibilities. Just make sure that if you do volunteer for another's work, you deliver what you've promised on a timely basis. Maintain a level of excellence on any extra work you volunteer for.

Become a liaison. Power and support accrue to those who become liaisons between their companies and other organizations. There are many ways of doing this. For instance, a mid-level manager at the large pharmaceutical company Pfizer developed an excellent method of achieving visibility and hence attracting supporters. He became the spokesman for the company in a series of public-service television ads. Some people seek to be quoted in trade journals so that they can achieve visibility and support within their company as well as outside it.

Becoming a company liaison has a subliminal effect on people both within the company and outside. They begin to perceive you as the primary representative of the company, and this public identification with the company can have powerful effects on your career. As you represent your company well in publications, at conferences, or in the media, you begin to be perceived as a winner.

Use your contacts to power. Utilize your contacts to powerful people. These contacts are themselves members of your supporting cast, who can help recruit more powerful people into your power base.

This is quite different from networking, which frequently is little more than the "powerless linking up with the impotent." What you want is real contact—social ties and professional connections—with people at the top of the ladder.

We spoke earlier of identifying individuals who regularly interface with those in power. They could be your immediate supervisors or peers. One of the best contacts is the secretary of the person whom you want to recruit as a supporter. The secretary's power exceeds his or her formal authority—one prominent example of the unreliability of the organizational chart as an indicator of real power.

Make yourself known to these potential contacts. Find out what their career goals are and how you can help them achieve those goals. Once they believe you will support them, they will be more willing to play the contact role to help you gain access to the person you want as a corporate sponsor.

Attend trade and professional meetings. Your participation in trade and professional associations can help you establish visibility in your company and throughout the industry. It also signals to your potential supporters that you are interested in professional growth.

If your potential supporters are members of the same associations, they will see you at meetings. If they don't belong, you could try more unusual approaches. One of my respondents felt frustrated that he wasn't moving up quickly enough. To accelerate his career progress, he ran for the presidency of a large trade association. As president he immediately moved the group's monthly meetings to his company's building. He then told the chairman of the company, "We're hosting a meeting of my organization, and I would just love it if you would stick your head in to say hello."

This was a great way of gaining visibility. When the boss dropped by, he would see that the manager was doing a good public relations service for the company. The boss would also observe him in a leadership role.

Use lunch hour to "power tryst." If you want to develop a supporting cast in a business organization, use the lunch hour to expand your contacts, to spend quiet time with those whose support you need. Dining with someone can become quite a democratic affair. So it may be worth your while to try to arrange even a working lunch with someone whose support you want. One technique is to schedule meetings so close to lunchtime that all concerned must extend the meeting into a working lunch. These invariably become more informal than the meeting itself and allow you to become known in a more personal way.

You may be helped by a corporate policy that facilitates your lunching with higher-ups. Hewitt Associates, for instance, utilizes a free-lunch policy to encourage employees to dine together and exchange information. Many companies have eliminated the executive dining room to increase communication between the ranks.

Don't be intimidated by the idea of initiating a conversation over lunch with a higher-up. Many managers are anxious to converse with those lower down the corporate ladder. They enjoy the camaraderie and informality of mealtime bantering.

Be a good sport. Many companies provide fitness centers, gyms, and running tracks for their employees. Such settings can provide excellent places for gaining visibility and acceptance.

One executive notes that the president of his company works out at the corporate fitness center. On occasion, some more opportunistic lower-level employee gets on the stationary bicycle beside the top man and starts sharing ideas about what the company should be doing. The president is "naturally going to talk to anyone on the next bicycle," this executive says.

Look for any opportunity to become familiar with people on a one-on-one situation. For instance, one of my respondents mentions a rising executive in the organization who plays tennis with the higher-ups. A superb athlete, he often beats them, and they remember his prowess. He is also leaving subtle hints in their minds that he is competent, aggressive, and in control.

Gary Wilson, the Disney Company's chief financial officer, has remarked that participation in sports provides a great background for business insofar as it teaches hard work and team play. You can well imagine how positively such an executive would react to an employee who participated in sports on or off the job site. He would assume that this employee is well prepared for corporate life and therefore worthy of support.

Company softball teams offer a great way to gain visibility. Socializing usually follows the game. This kind of relaxed atmosphere is an excellent way to meet prospective supporters.

Take advantage of informal gatherings. Many opportunities for expanding your work relationships occur at parties, social events, and company picnics. These events give potential sponsors among senior executives a more complete view of your talents. They also provide people with an opportunity to connect a name with your face. At the same time they allow you to further assess your potential supporters. Are they still as attractive to you outside of the corporate environment?

Not everyone agrees that the social aspect is integral to moving up and gathering support. Generally speaking, however, the higher up you want to go, the more social interaction is required for attracting the supporting cast. The more democratic the setting, the greater the chance that the difference in ranks between you and others will be diminished. As the perceived differences disappear, you have a greater chance to connect. Moving across levels of a hierarchy is a difficult challenge for anyone, no matter where you are in an organization.

Of course, you must be cognizant of your organization's unspoken rules. You don't want to transform what could be an advantage into a disaster. So, for instance, before attending a cocktail party, know your company's drinking code, dress standards, and concept of the "appropriate" companion. And watch your behavior! Even at informal company gatherings, you are still on display as an employee.

Chair a service committee. According to one senior manager, chairing a committee of a charitable or service organization makes sense as a way to enhance your visibility:

Developing contacts is not only a service to yourself. It is also perceived as a service to the organization. In our organization, if you hobnob with a president or vice president of another company, you become one more contact for your company.

The chairmanship of such a committee will not only help you score points with supporters but will also serve as a vehicle for attracting support across the industry.

Follow up initial contacts. Once you have made the acquaintance of a prospective supporter, follow up the contact with a phone call. Make it clear that you are following up because you want to maintain contact and truly help this person: "I was so thrilled to run into you the other day. Is there anything else I can help you with? Should we make an appointment to get together soon?"

You won't come across as pushy. In fact, you will appear to be a conscientious, concerned, and thorough person. Of course, people don't necessarily dislike pushy behavior if there is some substance underlying the aggressiveness. You want the person to understand that you are trying to add something of value to his storehouse of knowledge and make his job easier.

Successercize 4 offers some suggestions to help you increase your visibility within the work environment.

A Short Visibility Workshop

Achieving visibility is the way to recruit seniors into your supporting cast. Try some of these tips to increase your visibility and enhance your public persona in your organization.

1. At your next meeting, make at least two points or comments about the matters under consideration.

2. Volunteer for at least one key project, regardless of the extra time involved.

3. Invite to lunch at least one supervisor, manager, or senior executive.

4. Go to at least one extra organizational function, such as a holiday party, cocktail party, or after-work informal drink.

5. Interact with at least two supervisors, managers, or senior executives during office hours.

6. Hand deliver reports or other pieces of written work during the course of the day instead of sending them through normal channels. Try to initiate at least a brief (15 to 30 minute) discussion with the recipient of a report.

7. The next time you are asked to work late by a superior, do so.

8. Join at least one on-site club or extracurricular activity that entails at least some interaction with superiors.

9. Propose to your department or group at least one change in procedures or policy.

10. Make it known in informal conversation with a superior that you want a fuller explanation of promotion and training policy.

11. Volunteer for at least one business trip.

12. Draw attention to at least one of your accomplishments in the workplace.

How Do You Know Your Efforts Are Working?

Most of the time, you'll have ways of discovering whether your efforts to draw support are working. Of course, this assessment will be easier if you have recruited into your cast a trusted advisor who can regularly deliver news about management's ever-improving opinion of you. But without such a supporter, you must learn to read the signals from the environment.

Some signals are unambiguous. If you are being given more key assignments or increased responsibility, you have clear indications that you are being supported somewhere in the organization. As this begins to happen, be sure you find out from the person leading the project why you're being selected, and how important the project is to the organization.

On the other hand, you may succeed in your quest to achieve visibility but not know it. Perhaps you are being groomed for a future promotion or project by a supporter moving behind the scenes. Not knowing of your "secret admirers" can cause you career problems. For instance, if you don't know that you are viewed well, you might quit, transfer, or lower your performance level to meet what you think are management's poor expectations of you.

Rather than remaining in the dark, ask people in power,

at least your boss or supervisor, whether top management is aware of your accomplishments. Ask them to interpret ambiguous signs of career progress. For instance, what does a newly assigned project or assignment mean in terms of your ultimate career goals? Some projects are meant to test your competence. Of course, even when you are uncertain whether you are being observed, you should always exhibit energy, creativity, and a high standard of excellence in your performance. Assume that you are being judged every step of the way.

SUPPORT FROM BELOW

Your supporting cast must not be limited to those ahead of you in the organization. You also need the support of your subordinates.

Tim, a successful entrepreneur, discovered how essential it is to have a broad base of support. Like so many entrepreneurs, Tim is finding that he needs cooperation and goodwill from everyone who affects the future of his business, including secretaries, support personnel, and his sales people.

You can only go as far as the people below will let you. The more efficiently they work, the better you as a manager will perform. If you don't have their cooperation, you could find your career in dire straits.

Your ability to work with subordinates is a significant indicator of your potential to move up the corporate ladder. What people throughout the company think of you is to a great extent conditioned by the comments that emerge from the lower ranks. Subordinates can be your best public relations specialists—or your worst. If the people you supervise think you are rough around the edges or not a team player, their comments can slow your career.

Subordinates can also be a source of valuable information. Rumors as well as hard facts abound at a company's lower levels. Subordinates can tell you how policies are received, how hard people are working, and what the morale level is. They can also serve as early warning signals on who's about to quit, who wants a transfer, who is upset about not being promoted. Most important, they can give you reports on what the lower levels think of your management style and policies.

In short, you need a loyal group of subordinates. Unfortunately, many of us think that those who work under us will follow us merely because we control their career progress. But obeisance doesn't imply support. Real support from below is earned by helping others grow in their jobs, giving them credit for a job well done, and letting them share in your success.

Build your workers' self-esteem. Mary Kay Ash, president and founder of the large cosmetic corporation Mary Kay, Inc., notes that the best way to obtain the commitment of employees is by building their sense of self-esteem. Clearly, to get the support of those below you, you must not only make them believe in you but also help them believe in themselves. Successful managers make their workers feel good about their abilities and their potential, by giving them attention, taking a personal interest in their career growth, and complimenting them when necessary.

Not everyone is skilled at making others feel good about themselves. Many managers lack support from below because they are unable to let their workers know that their contributions are valued. If you find yourself choking on a compliment, you will have problems making others feel good about their accomplishments. However, this is a skill you can learn, perhaps from your own advisors.

One way of improving your workers' self-image is to set reasonably high expectations. As they begin to meet these standards, they will begin to respect themselves more, and they will see you as the source of this new self-esteem.

Most important, you must listen carefully to the individual, an art we will explore in Chapter 8. The listening process is critical, for without it you cannot learn about others' needs, complaints, dreams, ambitions, excuses, and justifications. When you "turn off" to them, you are in essence telling them that they are worthless.

Listen to your subordinates' suggestions about how a job should be done. Some managers hold meetings to inform only—a one-way process—and then wonder why their people do not support their efforts. Staff meetings that allow for individual expression of opinion are crucial. Employees' self-image improves as they feel more in control, and the better they feel about themselves, the greater the chance that they will join your supporting cast.

Develop loyalty. Naturally you would like to develop a loyal staff, one that will back you in bad times, cover for you in an emergency, and put in extra hours if necessary to help you complete a project.

Developing a sense of loyalty in people who work for you is directly related to their perception that they will receive some benefit. The development of loyalty is a long-term process, one that should commence long before you need a specific task done. Loyalty is built gradually, by doing people favors and by showing gratitude. Be meticulous about saying thank you, giving a pat on the back, paying overtime, and giving compensatory time off. Workers must know their extra help will be acknowledged, and that overall impression starts early in your relationship. As one manager says:

> If this project is to start in July, the question is what were you doing with them last October. Were you available, were you concerned, were you asking them what they needed in order to do their job? Were you saying to

them, "You seem swamped right now, let me see what I
can do to help you"?

In other words, you have to take care of employees long
before you want them to take care of you. Of course, when
you are granting your subordinates these early favors, you
might subtly remind them that "maybe you can help me out
sometime."

Workers quickly pick up on your character traits and decide whether you are worth their loyalty. If you are a good
communicator who is viewed as patient and competent, those
below you will believe that you deserve their support.

Demonstrate trust. Your workers will support you to the
extent that they feel you trust their competence and character.
If you give employees the impression that you think they are
dishonest, incompetent, or both, do not be surprised if they
live down to your expectations.

There are many ways for you to tell your workers that you
trust them to carry out their jobs. You can keep them informed about upcoming policies and procedures. You can
share data with them that they ordinarily wouldn't be privy to.

Most important, don't look over your workers' shoulders.
If you do, they'll assume that you don't believe they can fully
function in their assignments.

Become a people developer. Another method of developing support from below is to convey through your attitude
and actions that you are interested in more than just your
subordinates' contribution to your projects or departmental
goals. You are also interested in their personal and professional growth. Once people feel that you are a partner in *their*
quest for success, they become more willing to help you
achieve your goals. This means you have to get personally
involved. You can show them the organizational ropes, help

them improve their skills, enroll them in courses and seminars, help them improve their presentation of self.

Of course, it is helpful to have the best people as your lower-level supporters. In the words of one human-resources manager:

> You should try to determine who are the really outstanding contributors in your organization, regardless of their level. Those should be the people you want on your team.

Naturally, the smaller the organization, the easier it is to spot key performers.

Get your people some exposure. Your subordinates will appreciate any efforts on your part to get them known around the organization. You can mention their names to key corporate figures, credit them in reports, or bring them into key committee meetings. Some managers try to get their employees assigned to interfunctional task forces where they will be exposed to senior people in the organization. Any time you are involved in a group project, make sure you share the success with your subordinates. As one manager says:

> In a project, from the very beginning I would make sure to publicize to the higher-ups the names of the people involved in the project, so that ultimately the success, or the failure of the project, is a shared experience.

Any of these actions will be a sure indication to subordinates that you are concerned about their career growth.

Make your workers feel like your peers. Some executives feel that the best way to develop support from below is to dispense with the superior-subordinate relationship completely. In other words, the manager endeavors to make the employee feel like a coequal, a partner. This is the message of management guru Tom Peters in his books *In Search of Excellence* and *A Passion for Excellence*. To gain support for their policies and their careers, managers must get out of their offices and begin to "wander around" the workplace, to make themselves more accessible to those below them and to act more like their workers' peers.

One senior executive was particularly conscious of wanting the employees of a manufacturing plant he supervised to feel at home with him:

> I wanted to know as much as possible about my people, and not just in general, but the facts—their health, their families—making them know that I respected them as individuals.

Because he would go out of his way to initiate contact with the workers, they eventually perceived him not so much as a boss but as a friend. Their high productivity was a result of the fact that they were working for someone they genuinely liked and were respected by.

Keep your workers' secrets whenever possible. Whether we are discussing relationships with subordinates or higher-ups, one lesson is the same: If you keep someone's secret under your hat, you will earn his confidence.

Your workers may confide in you any number of things: problems they are having at work, fears they have about their performance, even the fact that they are having an affair. The reason they tell you these secrets may be simply to get them off their chest, or to seek your advice or assistance. They certainly don't expect you to reveal these confidences to others.

Once they see you as trustworthy, they are more likely to become your supporter.

Be authoritative without being authoritarian. One of my respondents noticed that she received more support from her employees when she finally learned to be authoritative without being authoritarian. She learned to be a source of knowledge and direction rather than giving orders and dictating policy.

People respond to those they perceive as respecting them. When a manager treats people like children, they respond as such, becoming stubborn, uncooperative, and less willing to act autonomously.

DON'T FORGET YOUR PEERS

We have spent most of this chapter discussing your relationship with superiors and subordinates. However, you also need the support of your peers to achieve your goals. Peers can serve as conduits to those in positions of power, can give you advice on how to get ahead, and often play the valuable roles of cheerleader, celebrator, constructive critic, and esteem builder.

Many of my respondents claim that their peers' chief contribution is to provide an invaluable source of information. Without the support of your peers, it is difficult to acquire knowledge of disparate functions and fields, information you need to move ahead in your organization. According to one executive who worked his way up from engineer to plant manager to senior executive:

> With this network you can expand what you know, so that you have a finger on what is going on. I work in

engineering, but through my peer networks I was able
to keep my eye on what was going on in sales, marketing, and in personnel.

Many of the techniques mentioned throughout this chapter will help you recruit peers into your supporting cast. The
one factor that may be different in your relationship with
peers is that at some point you may begin to surpass them in
the company. You are then faced with the problem of how to
retain them in your supporting cast while you pass them by.
We will deal with this special topic in Chapter 10.

DO WOMEN HAVE A HARDER TIME GAINING SUPPORT?

My research leaves no doubt that women in business still
have a tougher time gaining support than men do. In spite of
economic and professional gains, in the world of business
and in many of the professions women are still plagued by
traditional female occupational stereotypes, such as secre-
tarial or lower-level clerical roles. Many subliminal elements
affect women's chances of gaining support. In the general life
experience of many executives, women usually play the role
of daughter, wife, or mother. While these are all positive roles
in the nonbusiness environment, if a woman's superiors see
her only in terms of these images, they may have a problem
relating to her as an equal in the business world.

In the face of these stereotypes, it is not surprising that
many women are puzzled about the correct way to act in
positions of power. How, for instance, do they convey a relaxed yet powerful image, while still maintaining control and
authority? These seemingly conflicting images make it difficult
for many women to gather the support of people in power.

All of these factors can also create problems for the woman attempting to get support from subordinates, who are quick to sense a superior's discomfort with power. As a consultant and organizational sociologist, I have the opportunity to observe the behavior of those in positions of power. Male senior executives are likely to emit signals that say "I belong here" and "I am comfortable with my power." At high-level meetings, they sit in relaxed positions and respond to subordinates' questions in a friendly, easy-going manner.

Many women executives I have observed exhibit traits more typical of outsiders or neophytes. They appear tense, guarded in their responses, and seem uncomfortable with holding and using power.

As a woman, if you want to gain the support of subordinates, you must learn to be comfortable with power and to relax with responsibility. Many of the hints earlier in this chapter about becoming familiar with members of the power structure on a one-to-one basis should help you feel more comfortable with exercising the power you have gained through your supporting cast.

One other point should be addressed here. Many of the women I have interviewed, in business and academia, express concern about the sexual aspects of the support dynamic. Many women have been dismayed to find that senior executives who they thought were interested in them as colleagues were mainly, or at least partly, interested in them as potential girlfriends or sexual partners.

Women (and men who work for women bosses) may face this problem. How, they ask, did "I want to work with you" become "How about dinner some night"? There is no easy solution. The obvious answer to give to a senior who is combining flirtation with support is "no thanks." On the other hand, many women have expressed the fear that if they shut the door in this way, their career support will quickly disappear.

Women can deal with this problem in a variety of ways. They can make it clear that they are just not interested—by their manner, dress, conversation. Some let the person know they are unavailable—that they are married or otherwise involved. In this way they feel that any support that is forthcoming from seniors is unadulterated (pun intended).

This does not mean that a woman should create obstacles between herself and senior male executives, or elicit support only from females. It means that she should recognize the sexual potential and establish ground rules she is comfortable with in order to build the supporting cast she desires.

WHERE DO YOU GO FROM HERE?

If, after trying the above suggestions, you still have a problem developing a supporting cast at work, I would suggest that you consider some possible culprits.

Some people seem to have a difficult time connecting with the power structure. Sometimes people's attitudes, not their ability, stand as a stone wall between them and success. In short, they have difficulty establishing alliances not because they lack the abilities to perform but because they just don't like working with and depending on others. They feel that the most worthwhile accomplishments are the ones achieved without the assistance of others.

If this sounds familiar, perhaps you should be on your own, working outside of an organizational hierarchy. Ronald, in becoming an independent management consultant, decided to go it alone after he realized that his need for autonomy and his independent spirit would undermine his attempts to make alliances in a structured work environment. He just didn't feel suited to corporate life.

He soon discovered, of course, that even entrepreneurs need supporting casts to succeed. But as an entrepreneur he has a greater choice of whom he incorporates into his supporting cast. He is not limited to a particular supervisor or specific senior executive. He has a greater latitude in whom he decides to align himself with.

If you are going to pursue a career in an organization, your success depends on your willingness to cooperate and enter into supportive relationships. In the modern corporation, isolation is the worst form of self-sabotage. You must take a more proactive stance to exchange information and develop a strong, loyal supporting cast. Use the suggestions in this chapter to develop your networks and garner support from superiors, subordinates, and peers. Learn to read the power structure, attract the movers and shakers, develop the loyalty of your subordinates, and surround yourself with peers who can help you achieve your goals.

There is one other point to keep in mind. A penetrating article in *Business Week* makes it apparent just how seriously many American companies are beginning to view teamwork as a positive organizational force. General Motors, Xerox, and other companies are increasingly adopting the Japanese model of cooperation and teamwork, "jointness," to move their companies ahead. Boeing, Ford, GE, and Procter & Gamble have all moved to the "team concept" for increasing productivity.

This being the case, adopting the supporting cast principle is a most appropriate way to help you achieve your goals. Your spirit of cooperation and teamwork will put you in alignment with the coming business philosophy of corporate America.

CHAPTER SIX

Sabotage, and How You Can Deal with It

Not everyone will want to become your supporter. With some people you just will not have the chemistry needed for support to be possible. These individuals pose no threat to your future and should not be of concern.

There is another group, however, that does require your close attention. These are the people who, for whatever reason, want to see you fail. Unlike those individuals who are indifferent to you, these people do have an interest in your future—they want to disrupt it. Either overtly or covertly, they may attempt to undermine your efforts to achieve success. Those who deliberately try to impede your progress are saboteurs.

Every situation has a darker side—and in human relationships, the negative counterbalance to support is sabotage. Sabotage is any attempt by an individual or group to subvert someone else's success and growth. Whether conscious and malicious or unconscious and inadvertent, sabotage can occur anywhere: on the job or in our personal lives. Parents may inadvertently sabotage their own children, through jealousy, ignorance, or simply misguided instincts. Moreover, sabotage is not always active. It can consist in the absence of action—withdrawal of support when it is most needed.

Sabotage takes many forms. At work, saboteurs may attempt to steal your ideas or make sure that your proposals never see the light of day. Or they may spread stories about how your contribution to the company is of limited value. On a personal level saboteurs may try to convince you that your accomplishments are merely ordinary. They may undermine your self-confidence, attack your appearance or ethnic background.

Sabotage is an unpleasant fact of life. Once you accept that not everyone wishes you well, you can take the necessary steps to lessen your vulnerability to subversive attack. While this is not a simple procedure, there are strategies you can adopt in order to overcome attempts to block your success.

THE CADENCE OF SABOTAGE

Most people are fairly satisfied to simply live their lives and do their jobs. They get along with others and would consider it utterly foreign to harm someone else in order to get ahead or feel fulfilled. However, there is a small minority who will not hesitate to undermine others in their attempts to succeed. Such people may make an intentional and determined effort to subvert your ego, unhinge your career, and stifle your personal development.

Saboteurs work most effectively among those who have little knowledge of the existence of this malevolent force. They generally work surreptitiously, neither announcing their intention to derail your career nor revealing their tactics. The key to controlling sabotage, then, is learning to recognize its symptoms and confront its perpetrators. Sabotage has a certain cadence, a characteristic rhythm. The more skilled you become at recognizing it, the less power it will exert over your life.

Sometimes sabotage is administered so subtly that we are not even aware we are being undermined. In fact, the people involved in ego subversion are often those we trust most. I have seen countless examples of people who unwittingly turn in a crisis to the very people who in fact are trying to sabotage them. By the same token, many of us have a hard time differentiating friendly advice from sabotage. Good supporters often supply us with constructive criticism, but in our darker hours we might mistake this for attempted sabotage.

Sabotage and constructive criticism are worlds apart in their intention. The constructive critic wants you to improve; the saboteur wants you to fail. One good indicator of the difference is their reaction to your success. The constructive critic will help you celebrate; the saboteur will find a way to diminish your achievement.

Learn to distinguish criticism from sabotage. After all, your success depends on people who will alert you to those instances when you take the wrong path, who will warn you when you adopt self-destructive behavior. Successercize 5 will help you learn how to distinguish friend from foe.

Spotting Saboteurs

The following questions should help you determine whether any individuals in your social circle or work environment are actual or potential saboteurs. The more "yes" responses, the greater the likelihood that this person is a saboteur.

INDIVIDUAL

RELATIONSHIP

1. The last time you told this person something good about yourself, did he or she seem to be not particularly happy?   Y   N

2. Does it seem to be not particularly important to this person that you succeed?   Y   N

3. Overall, does this person seem to be really not on your side?   Y   N

4. Does this person often express jealousy toward you?   Y   N

5. Does this person seem threatened by your accomplishments?   Y   N

6. Does this person often talk about you behind your back?   Y   N

7. Have you noticed that this person tends to "rub it in" when you fail?   Y   N

8. Has this person intentionally done things to   Y N
   obstruct your accomplishing your goals?

   If the person listed at the top of the page elicits six or
more "yes" responses, he or she is most likely playing the
saboteur in your life. People are often surprised when
"friends" whom they think of as supporters show up as
saboteurs.

TYPES OF SABOTEURS

Although saboteurs come in countless varieties, the effect on
your career, and your self-esteem, is always the same. If you
are not equipped to deal with this person, a scrape with a
saboteur could put your future happiness in jeopardy.

The Obvious Saboteur

The easiest type of saboteur to spot is the one who openly
announces that he or she is out to undermine your career,
subvert your self-confidence, and in general create problems
for you.

   A producer at a local TV station recounted to me how
she had been assigned a college student as an intern. The
student, who couldn't have been more than 19, informed the
producer early on, "I want your job." Of course, the intern was
in no position at that time to make good on her threat. But
due to the lack of job security in the media world, her state-
ment made the producer rather concerned.

   In a sense, the young intern was doing a favor for the
producer, herself only 24. She was telling her up front that she
was going to do whatever it took to undermine the producer's

position. The student was an obvious saboteur, someone who believed her actions could be justified if her intentions were known.

Saboteurs of this type make no secret of their intentions to obstruct your progress. In spite of the open warning, the saboteur's actions may be so upsetting that your work may be disrupted.

The Friendly Enemy

Unfortunately, most sabotage is not as transparent as this. For sabotage to be really effective, it's best that the victim have no inkling of what's about to hit.

I know of one published author who seems to be the perfect supporting cast member. She provides networking opportunities for others, is generous with valuable career information, and provides her friends with contacts. But when the people she is helping begin to succeed, threatening to equal her success and status, she subtly begins to undermine their self-confidence and question their abilities. Many of the people whom she emotionally sabotages listen to her advice as if it is actually constructive criticism.

Many people you will meet are this type of saboteur. Even when they seem to be praising you, they are really trying to convince you of your own imperfection. They have mastered the art of the left-handed compliment—ambiguous statements, such as "You've really improved your appearance lately," which are intended to make you feel not more self-confident but more uncertain of yourself.

The Backstabber

The backstabber is a saboteur with whom you may have minimal contact at most. This individual does his work behind the scenes.

You may become the victim when some other employee's protector wants to push his or her favorite into a top position. In order to promote that person, the saboteur may have to impede your progress. You will find out that you are the object of a backstabber's attention when he begins to circulate negative "facts" about you, gets you removed from key projects, and makes sure his favored employee attends all the key meetings.

There's nothing personal in this. In fact, if you and the saboteur ever met, you might get along just fine. However, the backstabber has priorities, and you are not one of them. In fact, you are an obstruction to his favorite's progress.

People backstab for any number of reasons, which we will review next. If you do not confront these people, either directly or through others, and stop them, their efforts may damage your career.

WHY PEOPLE SABOTAGE

When we find that someone on the job or in our personal life is spreading lies about us, is trying to ensure that we don't get promoted, is withdrawing emotional and technical support just when we seem to need it most, we first want to know why. By understanding their motivations we can more effectively defend ourselves against saboteurs.

They want to get ahead. Often, there is little mystery surrounding the motivation to sabotage. As one human-resources executive puts it: "There are people out there who believe that the world is a finite pie, and they can only get ahead by taking others' shares away from them."

They may simply want your position and are trying to get you out of the way. While they harbor no negative feelings toward you personally, they must ensure that you look bad, or don't get credit for any accomplishments that might lead to your advancement.

This sabotage usually manifests itself subtly. The saboteur typically remains friendly and cooperative until you appear to be in the way of his or her gaining a good job, office, or project. At such a point, they suddenly withdraw their support or overtly attempt to undermine you.

They just don't like the idea of someone else doing well. A number of people engage in sabotage simply because it bothers them that others are making personal and career progress. Such people probably believe they have reached a point in their careers in which they can go no further.

According to one engineer, the people to be wary of are those who have few opportunities for advancement.

> They don't have a degree, so their own mobility is limited. I've come across a couple of occasions where people have openly expressed resentment to me over my promotion to senior technician.

How do such types assuage their own sense of failure? They may withhold critical information on a project, respond blankly to your request for advice even when they have the answers to your questions, and display any variety of "passive-aggressive" behaviors that all add up to sabotage.

They don't like you. A certain amount of sabotage can be accounted for only by the fact that someone feels a need to harm you and is willing to expend time and energy satisfying that desire. The person may dislike you because of some imagined slight or insult. Or you may remind someone of a despised parent or the wife who left him. If such unconscious factors are at play, you may be in for some rough sledding, since this person sabotages you for no perceptible gain.

They see you as a loser. There are some people—and these include family and friends—who simply have a low opinion of your ability to accomplish anything. They may like you very much as a person, but for some reason they have an image of you as inherently incompetent.

If you value their opinion in general, there is a good chance you may accept their view of you. Their lack of faith in you weakens your resolve and diminishes your chances of becoming successful.

One entrepreneur I interviewed could have allowed his friends' lack of confidence in his ability to start a business sabotage his quest for success. They felt obliged to inform him that he would probably fail miserably in his attempts to build a business. They presented him with several reasons why he would fail—the market was weak, he didn't have enough of a financial cushion—but the overall message they conveyed was that he just wasn't talented enough to make it as an entrepreneur. Fortunately, his wife played a strong esteem-builder role to sustain him through this period.

They have emotional problems. Some people's tendency to sabotage others has nothing at all to do with personality conflicts or competitive situations. Their destructive tendencies stem from their severe emotional problems.

They may be sufficiently coherent to secure employment but unbalanced enough to make the life of everyone in the office miserable. Who they dislike, and why they dislike them, seems to have no rhyme or reason. They can unsettle an entire department by constant complaints and negative comments to top management. These complaints may center around other workers' performance, lack of commitment to the firm, or uncooperative spirit. This type of saboteur can get others fired, transferred, or demoted.

Fortunately, people like this are usually so blatant in their attempted sabotage that the entire organization sees them for what they are. This awareness helps immeasurably in counter-acting the effects of their sabotage.

SABOTAGE AT WORK

Any corporation or organization that is in any way political contains the potential for sabotage. All it takes is the right people to start the action. Anyone, from your superiors or peers to your own workers, can sabotage you on the job.

Sabotage from Above

You may find yourself in a situation in which your supervisor or senior manager likes to abuse power and has a need to demonstrate control. This person could feel threatened by your career progress, a recent promotion, or a raise, and do everything possible to subvert your progress.

This insecure boss may steal your original concepts or take credit for your work. Some executives contend that this liberal "borrowing" should not be a concern as long as you know that your boss truly values you. I disagree. The boss may justify this pilferage because "that's the way we do things around here," but that doesn't mean it won't have some delete-rious effects on your career.

A boss can also sabotage you by putting you in positions in which you are bound to fail—a job you don't have the training for, or a position for which you are ill-prepared.

You should be aware of several danger signs that may mean people above you in the organization—be they direct supervisors or senior managers—are trying to derail your ca-reer. One indication is that you are not chosen for key projects or are bumped from the ones you are already on. Another is that in spite of your excellent job performance, you may be viewed negatively by the powers that be. If this is the case, you must first engage in some serious self-examination. Is your work really as good as you like to think it is? Are you playing by the company rules? Are you a team player?

If, after honest self-evaluation, you conclude that your job performance is not being adequately appreciated, you can conclude that sabotage is a factor.

A word of caution is needed here. Even if your immediate supervisor is not attempting to upend you career, other superiors may attempt sabotage. In that case you may need your boss's protection. A politically weak supervisor, while not acting the part of saboteur himself, may not be able to protect you from other sharks in the corporate waters. In that case, the weak supervisor can be as harmful to your career as the more forthright saboteur.

Sabotage from Below

How do you know when you are being sabotaged by the people who work for you? They may cause delays in a project, so that you miss a deadline or reach it only at the eleventh hour. Or they may take information that you have generated and distort it, or report what you say while casting it in the worst possible light. When you need information to complete a proposal, they may give you only the data you specifically request, no more. They may leave out some critical fact that you need to know.

One human-resources director has a good insight into sabotage from below.

> You may ask someone to do a project, and ask him to answer three critical questions. As he becomes involved in it, he realizes that even if your critical questions get answered, you've overlooked something major. If employees don't volunteer the information that you are mak-

ing a mistake in your analysis, they are probably sabotaging you. Then, to cover themselves, they may volunteer the information after the project backfires.

In effect, your subordinates have deliberately helped you make a wrong decision. The worst part of the above scenario is that since, strictly speaking, the employee gave you what you asked for, you cannot even accuse him of undermining your efforts. Often the saboteur simply responds that he misunderstood your priorities in the assignment. "If you had told me what you wanted, I would have been happy to do it," he will explain.

Keep one thing in mind: Subordinates are in no position to express resentment openly. You, not they, have the power. To an extent you control the rewards and dispense the punishments. Therefore, subordinates often undermine you passively, secretly, making this type of sabotage difficult to detect and overcome.

One of my respondents mentioned that she has seen subordinates use informal arenas, such as parties and lunchtime, to say negative things to superiors regarding their boss. Because the comments are proffered in semisocial situations, the higher-up may not have the opportunity to ask in-depth questions about the specifics of the charges. But these whispers and rumors add up to subliminal sabotage.

When are subordinates most prone to sabotage you? Here are some key organizational scenarios that should make you particularly wary.

- You have just been hired from elsewhere and are considered an outsider by your subordinates.

- You are replacing someone who was a favorite of the subordinates, someone whose departure is deeply resented by your new charges.

- You have been promoted from the ranks and are now supervising your former peers.

- Worse, you may be put in charge of the very person who everyone feels should have gotten the position instead of you.

While the above scenarios are a tipoff to potential sabotage from below, the only sure way to determine whether you are being sabotaged is to have a good network of "information outposts," advisors and other supporters strategically placed around the organization. No CEO could run a company without such supporters.

One general manager explained to me how he nips in the bud sabotage from below.

> When that type of thing starts happening around me, I know I have people close to me who can come forth with the information early enough so I can deal with the problem before it gets out of control.

Information is one of your greatest weapons in your fight against sabotage.

How to Deal with Sabotage on the Job

Whether sabotage is emanating from above you or from the ranks, you must deal with it. First you must diagnose who is sabotaging you, why, where, when, and how. You may have to do much information gathering, but it will be well worth the effort.

Then you must act on this information. If it turns out that someone is sabotaging you, there are several responses you can take. Each has its pros and cons. You must assess the saboteur, the situation, and your own ability to deal with this phenomenon to determine which approach will be most effective.

If you think you are being sabotaged, don't wait! Sabotage does not go away on its own. The pollyannaish view that because you would never hurt another's career you are somehow exempt from being on the receiving end of anyone's ill will is the first step to disaster. Take the following steps to meet the crisis head-on.

Find out what's happening. First get the particulars of the sabotage situation by seeking information from people you really trust, people you know are not in collusion with the saboteur(s). For instance, numerous female corporate managers I've interviewed have had to act quickly when they heard that their reputations were being smeared by some competitor who claimed they were having a sexual liaison with the boss. They had to go to their information outposts to track down exactly who was sabotaging them, and to find out how widespread these rumors had become.

Activate your support network. Once you know the extent of the potential damage, enlist the help of your advisors, public relations specialists, and sponsors to defeat the saboteur. If necessary, have your supporting cast members talk to the saboteur, or his or her supervisor. Some sponsors may intercede and have the target of the sabotage promoted out of harm's way.

This is a major reason you need a strong supporting cast of loyal well-wishers in your organization to come to your aid when necessary.

Confront the person. If you are confident of your strength in an organization, you may want to confront the saboteur directly. You should not do this unless you have the facts surrounding the saboteur's actions and are sure that key members of the organization will support you in your accusations.

A skilled saboteur may never admit to being involved in sabotage. He may be very good at covering his tracks. You may not be able to prove in a direct confrontation that this person is involved in any subterfuge at all. But you will be putting him on notice that if the sabotage doesn't stop, you will defend yourself.

Make sure the confrontation is done in private. You don't want your actions to backfire by having an open battle over the sabotage. This could give the saboteur an opportunity to make remarks publicly that he or she was making surreptitiously before. Also, you want to give your nemesis a chance to withdraw from this confrontation with no loss of face. The only way to accomplish this is in a one-on-one discussion.

Go over the person's head. You can tell the saboteur's boss what is occurring: that the person is stealing your ideas, for example, or has erased your computer program. But to pull this off successfully you need to have as much evidence as you would if you were in court. If you can't prove your case, you will look foolish, or even malicious, both to the saboteur's boss and to the organization in general.

Again, the issue of privacy is central. If you go over someone's head, do it quietly. Otherwise you may look like you can't handle your own battles.

STOPPING SABOTAGE BEFORE IT STARTS

There are several ways to preempt sabotage before it even begins.

Recognize the potential for resentment. The person most vulnerable to sabotage is the one who imagines that his every success will be greeted with applause by peers he passes by on the organizational chart. This is naive. People vary in their responses to others' success. You must continually strive to make your own achievements somehow valuable to others.

Hire supporters. It's easier to hire a supporter than to transform a potential enemy into an ally. Many executives deal with the sabotage issue by making sure that the people they bring on board believe in them and will be loyal to them. This is why a new manager brought in from outside the company may quickly encircle himself with newly hired employees. People usually think of this as cronyism, an "old-boys network" ploy. In fact, the manager wants to be surrounded by people he knows will support him and not undercut his efforts.

Establish credibility. You should always make it known to others that you have the education and skill to do the job and that you deserve any promotions coming your way. Let peers and others know exactly how you got your new job. While the actions you take in establishing credibility in and of themselves may not make those around you members of your supporting cast, they might dissuade your co-workers from seriously considering sabotage.

By establishing credibility you may be able to prevent one problem mentioned earlier: your boss claiming your work as his or her own. My respondents suggest a variety of cures for this form of sabotage.

One younger manager makes sure that everyone she deals with while producing a report—associates, researchers, superiors—knows that it is *she* who is putting this report together, not anyone else.

Others have subtler ways of preventing their boss from usurping their work. They may ask to be credited as co-author of the project report, so that the organization will be aware that the project was a joint effort. One man prevents his boss from stealing the limelight by making sure that all of his key accomplishments at work are documented—in company newsletters, memos, and at meetings.

When you hand in a report to your boss, one manager advises, you should have your name clearly on the cover sheet. The boss then will have to remove the cover sheet to substitute his or her name on your work—in effect saying, "No mistake about it: I ripped off the cover sheet with your name on it and had it retyped with my name."

Make and maintain alliances. You must develop support networks to create a wall of invulnerability around yourself to discourage sabotage. The stronger you look, the less you will be subject to attack. A person known to have a widespread supporting cast is much less likely to be sabotaged than the loner.

Don't make an easy target. Regardless of their motivation and how much they perceive they will gain, saboteurs will not act against you if they think you are strong enough to resist. A victimizer needs a victim. If you seem like an easy target, you actually invite sabotage. A weak self-image may place you in the victim role. The stronger you appear, the less likely you will be to be perceived as an easy target.

EGO SUBVERSION

Whether on the job or in your personal life, you could be confronted with a far more insidious type of sabotage: ego subversion. Just at the point when you are about to embark on a crucial project or take a new job, someone places doubts in your mind about your ability. Ego subversion is the act of overtly or subtly undermining someone's trust in his or her own judgment, appearance, taste, or ability.

Ego subversion is the exact opposite of esteem building. Esteem builders help us develop our self-confidence, make us feel competent and worthy of success. But some people, even those in our immediate circle, will for whatever reasons attempt to undermine our sense of competence.

Some of us are more vulnerable than others to this particular type of subversion. It is a question of how weak our self-image is in the first place and how much we value the person acting against us. If our self-esteem is low, we may unconsciously seek out those who will lower it even further, thus replaying the dynamics of our childhood relationships with parents.

Some people unconsciously undermine others, with words and innuendo. It's not that they are acting in a consciously spiteful or negative manner. Others, however, know full well how ego subversion can weaken an opponent.

Most of us assume that most people are supporters. And, in fact, the majority do help friends in need and contribute to their growth. But some people are less charitable in their intentions. They may see someone else's gain as their loss, and do whatever is necessary to derail that person's career progress, or to stop the progress before it even begins.

Ego subversion is tricky to spot, because it often looks and sounds like constructive criticism. The difference between constructive criticism and ego subversion is a crucial one. Constructive criticism is intended to strengthen you. It provides you with essential feedback about your actions, plans, and ideas for personal growth. By contrast, ego subversion is intended to weaken you. The saboteur makes you question the very areas in which you feel most vulnerable, thus undermining your self-confidence and self-esteem.

When presented with feedback, you must honestly assess the criticizer's motives. Does he or she stand to gain if you fail? Is there competition between you, direct or indirect?

Learning to distinguish between constructive criticism and ego subversion is an essential skill for both personal and professional success. A first step in this direction is to be suspect of unsolicited feedback. You must also avoid giving more credence to others' perceptions than you do to your own.

This, by the way, is one of the reasons you need to be especially careful in choosing members of your supporting cast. If you are inadvertently recruiting saboteurs into your immediate circle, you must ask why. Redirect your attention to early childhood patterns. Often, it is parents who first pulled the ego-support rug out from under us. We may be unconsciously repeating these early family patterns by choosing friends and lovers who replicate this behavior.

Favorite Targets of Vulnerability

If someone really wants to undermine your self-image, they need to know where you are most vulnerable. People who are really talented at undermining others' self-esteem seem to have an almost uncanny ability to quickly read another's personality and find the weak points. Here are some typical targets of vulnerability.

Competence. Many people feel insecure about their ability to compete, to perform, to excel. When you are in new surroundings, a supporter will try to build your self-image. A saboteur will try to subvert it.

In a work situation, a friendly saboteur may begin to suggest to you that you are really not cut out for the job—you don't have the talent, the know-how, the experience. If you are in the arts, a saboteur may play upon your doubts about your ability, the commercial potential of your work, or the originality of your ideas.

Gender. Sometimes it is more effective to attack what sociologists call ascribed characteristics—aspects we have absolutely no control over, such as gender.

Cynthia, an engineer, has experienced ego subversion

from co-workers who try to use her sex as a way of weakening her self-image. She has recently moved into a higher position, and there are those who resent her sufficiently to attempt to undermine her self-confidence. She would have received this promotion regardless of her sex. But most of her co-workers are aware that the company's affirmative-action policy mandates a certain number of females in key positions. In the hands of saboteurs, this policy becomes a weapon to undermine self-confidence and erode self-esteem. "People remind you of the existence of quotas," Cynthia says. "Maybe I'm just another token. I want to believe I got there on merit."

As an engineer, Cynthia has frequently confronted the attitude that women don't belong in the hard sciences, that women can never really understand engineering, mechanics, and theoretical physics. Hence, the questions at work about her worthiness for her new position feed on a preexisting image problem.

Ethnic group and race. Women aren't the only group vulnerable to ego subversion. Blacks, Hispanics, and other ethnic groups are easy targets of saboteurs. Sometimes, in order to undermine the self-esteem of a member of a minority, a saboteur may talk about the person behind his back, knowing full well that the comments will find their way to the person's ears. Other times they blatantly make direct ethnic or racial slurs. Even if these comments are made "jokingly," the effect is to remind others that the target of the remarks belongs to a group that is viewed unfavorably in the organization.

A good supporting cast can help a minority member in the fight against ego subversion by giving psychological and tactical assistance. Unfortunately, some minority individuals find it emotionally difficult to assemble a supporting cast because of the risk they perceive in relying on others.

One black manager I spoke to is in a typical minority situation. He is part of a management group in which only 6 of 72 vice presidents are nonwhite. He feels that blacks, if they are to move up, must find a way to negotiate through what is still a white corporate world. They must learn to build bridges and alliances. "The biggest problem for a minority is to learn how to trust others in the organization. But if you don't find people to rely on somewhere down the road, you may as well quit."

There is no doubt that race or nationality can be used to close people out of the corporate ranks. Fortunately, many of the blacks I spoke to have been able to use their success and career progress as a wedge against ego subversion. The better they perform, the more credibility they build in the company's eyes and, more important, in their own eyes. One manager has learned to live with the situation, and sees it improving. "I haven't let myself get beaten down by the race issue. And it's gotten better since I started."

Physical appearance. People often choose appearance as an object of sabotage. They may imply to us that we are not good looking enough, are dressed improperly, or are not stylish. We hear these digs so often that we may take little notice of them. However, they are often an effective method of ego subversion. Since much of our self-esteem is connected to our appearance, remarks directed at our physical makeup can become lethal weapons for a skilled saboteur.

For instance, recent surveys have discovered that a vast majority of people feel that they fall short of what they consider society's ideal of physical perfection. A person in this state of mind makes an easy victim. The saboteur who discovers that you are insecure about your weight, height, eye color, skin tone, or other bodily features may exploit those insecurities.

Handling Ego Subversion

Ego subversion is qualitatively different from other forms of sabotage. Unlike direct sabotage, ego subversion is usually a one-on-one contest in which someone is attempting to undermine your self-confidence.

Your ability to handle ego subversion is first and foremost linked to your self-concept. The weaker your self-esteem to begin with, the more vulnerable you are to ego sabotage. Perhaps you even feel drawn to people with negative opinions of you, because they reinforce your own negative self-assessment. By the same token, the stronger your self-image, the more you see yourself as inherently competent, the greater the chance you will discourage saboteurs.

Ego strength is usually derived from early childhood experiences. Although you cannot change what has already happened, you can use your knowledge of those experiences to understand how vulnerable you currently are to ego subversion. Perhaps you should review the material in Chapter 4 to assess your weak spots based on early childhood experience. Evaluate how strong your self-confidence is and how much effort you must put into countermanding the saboteur's nefarious influence.

The most passive response to ego subversion is to maintain contact with the subverters and accept the negative bits of information they throw your way. This may not sound like a very good choice, but you would be surprised how many people keep going back for more negative stimuli from friends and lovers.

Or, you can retain them as friends but ignore their attacks on your vulnerability. Some people deal with ego subversion by "tuning out" the negative person. If the subverter is someone in your immediate circle, you may decide that their opinions about you—and about everything else—are relatively worthless.

Or, you can eliminate them from your circle. This choice may seem the most difficult. While you can eliminate friends, you may have less freedom to divest yourself of ego subverters who are family members or co-workers.

If you are stuck with a subverter, you may have to confront the person directly. Tell them you no longer wish to hear their opinions regarding your chances of achieving success.

Sabotage is an uncomfortable aspect of life, but an inevitable one when people compete. It is better to recognize the potential for sabotage than to pretend it can't happen to you. If you are being sabotaged, you must confront the situation. There is no neutral ground when someone is trying to derail your career.

The potential for sabotage should in itself be a compelling reason for you to strengthen your supporting cast. You need image builders, not subverters. You should always strive to strengthen your relationship with the true well-wishers in your immediate circle, and minimize contact, when possible, with ego subverters.

CHAPTER SEVEN

Lovers and Other Supporters

Your closest personal relationships and the support you get from them are significant factors in your achieving success. The personal relationship probably most important to your ultimate success is that with your mate or lover.

Statistics reveal a correlation between a stable marital relationship and financial success. While the divorce rate in the United States hovers around the 50 percent mark, the most successful businesspeople (those in the $100,000-plus income bracket) have remarkably intact relationships. Only 4 percent of the males in this group, and 20 percent of the females, have been divorced.

A stable relationship with a mate definitely has career benefits. How many times do we hear of people who put their mates through college, medical school, or business school? Robert Wright, president of General Electric Financial Services division, is quick to acknowledge the role his wife, Suzanne, played in his educational attainment. She worked to put him through the University of Virginia Law School, and his law degree became his ticket into General Electric as a staff attorney.

Yet ironically, when most of us choose a mate, we don't concern ourselves with whether that person has the potential to support us in our life and career. Often, romantic love is uppermost in our minds. While these feelings are important, there are other questions we should ask about a mate or prospective life partner.

For instance, does this person offer the emotional support you need to succeed? Is your lover threatened by your success? Will he or she do what is necessary to make your goals easier to achieve? If you're not in a relationship now but are looking, do you consider the potential for support an important attribute in a prospective mate?

Many executives have told me that their spouse is the make-it-or-break-it link in their ultimate career success. This may come as a surprise to many people who seem to be getting along just fine without a mate, who feel that friends and colleagues provide whatever assistance is needed. Don't we converse with friends the same way we'd talk with a spouse? Can't acquaintances express sympathy in much the same way a husband or wife would?

While the answer to these questions is a qualified yes, there are many reasons why marriage partners make better supporters than friends and acquaintances. For one thing, the spouse relationship is fundamentally different because of the interdependence of both members. Each marriage partner has a real stake in the other's future. For as long as the marriage lasts, each mate's success or failure will positively or negatively impact the other.

Of course, this interdependence comes from inside as well as outside the partnership. The intensity of feeling between the couple, the value that each places on the other's opinion, and their physical relationship raise the emotional bond to a point not experienced in other close relationships. For better or for worse, your primary relationship can greatly affect your overall success.

How Your Mate Affects Your Success

The experiences of the people I interviewed for this book are testimony to the power a lover or mate has over one's ultimate achievements. As we look at the ways a mate can affect life and career, it will be useful for you to compare your current relationship with those discussed here. Later, in Successercize 6, you can evaluate how supportive your mate is.

The Mate as Esteem Builder

While mates and lovers do not usually impact our success on the job directly, they affect our professional careers in many ways. The most important indirect effect is in the role they play in helping us maintain a positive self-image.

In effect, the supportive spouse continues a role that we should have had during childhood: the esteem builder. A mate helps us confirm our basic belief in ourselves as worthwhile, competent human beings. Sometimes our mates pick up where our parents left off, continuing to help us expand our horizons. At other times they "re-parent" us, providing us with the esteem building we failed to receive consistently from parents and others early in life.

In their early career years, Susan and Michael both needed that esteem building. As writers, they faced the periodic trauma of dry periods, those times when every publisher and magazine editor seemed to be rejecting their work. This is enough to spark intense self-doubt in even the most talented person.

Susan remembers how they bolstered each other's self-esteem through what she calls "shared optimism." "I always like to think we believed in each other more than we believed in ourselves. We just had unlimited confidence in each other's talent—not in a Pollyanna way, but realistically."

The ability of two people to affirm each other's innate talent and competence is one of the most profound types of support they can give each other. If your mate or lover is performing this function, you have definitely chosen well.

The Mate as Cheerleader

There can be no greater cheerleader than a spouse or lover. (I will use the designation "mate" to refer to the most significant person in your life.) Because your mate knows where you are most vulnerable, he or she also knows how to cheer you on when you are feeling at your lowest. The supportive mate can help you feel optimistic instead of gloomy, remind you of past successes and upcoming challenges, and convince you of your ability to perform well.

The second marriage of tennis star Chris Evert to former Olympic gold medalist Andy Mill demonstrates well the role of mate as cheerleader. Evert retired from the game in the fall of 1989, but recounted in a *Ms.* magazine article earlier that year how her husband's acceptance of her as a person, not just a tennis player, helped her deal with the defeats that came more frequently as her career neared its end. Instead of raging at herself for losing, she approached defeat with level-headed calm. When she lost a match, Mill reminded her that there would be other chances for victory. Perhaps, through the benefit of his own experience, he understood the letdown that can accompany a maturing sports career. As a result, he was able to play the role of cheerleader perfectly in his wife's life.

Susan and Michael too are well aware of how to cheer each other on. After her career as a freelance writer, Susan became communications manager for a Fortune 500 company. Michael is a journalist with a major daily. Susan enjoyed Michael's cheerleading support as she struggled to develop her writing career. Now this need continues even stronger as she makes the difficult transition to a regimented schedule, rigid deadlines, and greater demands on her time. In addition to the support system she is building on her job, Michael gives Susan that special emotional buttressing that only a mate or lover can provide.

The experiences of these two couples typify what is different about today's support system. In traditional families until the last two decades, men were not expected to reciprocate the cheerleading role characteristically played for them by their wives. But things have definitely changed. Now males are expected to fulfill the cheerleader role for their mates— especially mates who work. Historically the recipients of nurturing, they are now learning to provide it as well. At the same time, men are learning that the bottomless reservoir of support their fathers may have received will not be available to them, as their wives' focus of attention shifts to their own careers.

This change in the relationship between the American male and female is as profound as it is subtle. When both work, both need nurturance and support. Both bring home the strains and pressures of the outside job environment. They may have to develop new behavioral strategies in order to provide support for each other. They may, for instance, have to learn to sense which partner needs the most nurturance, which one has the greater need to talk about their job that night.

If, like more than half the couples in America, you and your mate both work, you will find that your relationship will run more smoothly if you both expend the time and energy to be each other's cheerleaders—listen to the other's problems, bolster the other's confidence, and play the optimist when necessary. Each must be the other's source of emotional support—and you must do so while simultaneously dealing with the pressures of your own job.

Bear in mind that cheerleading may have a different meaning for each sex. Susan realizes that Michael does not support her in the same way she chooses to support him. When she comes home with a problem, she expects emotional cheerleading plus a bit of commiseration. Although Michael offers the mandatory pep talk, he is more concerned with straight-out problem solving. As Susan puts it,

> I think men tend more to be tacticians: "If that's your problem, do this." But I feel that sometimes you have to work through your feelings and let them come to a boil before you can take action.

More important, though, is the fact that they both are generous with their support—each spends the time to cheer the other on. By giving of yourself in this way, you are informing your mate that you really care. Often it is the act of giving, more than what is given, that makes one person value another's support.

Someone to Celebrate the Good Times

The person who helps you celebrate the good times is an important supporting cast member. There is nothing more anticlimatic than getting a raise, completing a project, or having a creative breakthrough with no one to share it with. A mate is the ideal supplier of this emotional compensation.

Celebration has symbolic value. It tells you that your mate has a vested interest in your success. It also enables you to reward your mate for the sacrifices he or she made in helping you reach this point. Consequently, an early sign that a relationship is on the skids is when one partner is indifferent to the other's victories.

Does Your Mate Share the Load?

A good measure of your relationship is the extent to which your mate will help you succeed in the achievement of your goals. One of the acid tests of a mate's support is the extent to which he or she shares the responsibilities of maintaining a household—helping with the laundry, housework, cooking, or errands. This type of support is especially important in the two-career family.

Susan's transition to work outside the home was made easier by Michael's technical support, especially in regard to taking care of the children. "He's filled in a lot for me at home. He gets up early with the kids so I can get to work early. He gets them dressed and ready for school."

This is a mutually beneficial relationship. They have had time conflicts but have managed to work them out. Hiring a housekeeper has helped, but someone has to supervise her hours and give her assignments.

Conflicting time demands, no doubt, put a strain on partners' ability to share responsibility. But if your priority is mutual support, you should be able to work out these conflicts.

Your Spouse Is Part of Your Public Persona

Most of us marry for love or emotional support; we rarely consider the effect a spouse may have on our public image. We don't realize how others judge us in terms of our mate's appearance, demeanor, and style.

As you move up the occupational ladder, people in your organization or profession increasingly view your spouse as an extension of your own image. Many people feel this is unfair. After all, you want to be appreciated for who you are, not who you married. But often your choice of spouse is seen as a reflection of your overall judgment.

Of course, if you are already married, the question is to what extent your mate can reflect positively on you when socializing with your colleagues. However, if you are in the process of looking for a mate, perhaps you may want to consider seeking someone who will help your career by being a worthy representative.

Most people select as mates those whom they are proud to introduce to bosses and colleagues. Unfortunately, however, some people outgrow their mate in terms of style. If this is happening in your marriage, you owe it to both of you to sit down with your mate and explore his or her willingness to play the corporate game with you, and the impact non-cooperation will have on your career.

Your Best Advisor

Your mate may be your best career and life counselor. Your mate may know your capabilities so well that he or she can help guide you in your career planning.

By acting as his counselor/advisor, Susan became a major force in Michael's success. Although he thought that his major strength was photography, Susan believed that writing was his real talent. She urged him to make the transition into professional journalism.

Her encouraging words led him to try a career change. He became a writer for a string of weeklies, and eventually his interest in writing overtook his desire to be a photographer. Susan believed in his unlimited creativity. She says, "I always felt that the sky was the limit. He just had to find out what he wanted to do. I maybe helped to channel some of that energy."

Does your mate act as a career advisor? The most productive and giving relationships are ones in which each partner helps the other to find his or her niche in the occupational sphere.

Your Mate and Self-Actualization

Ultimately, the right mate helps you become a better person in all areas, not only career. The support emanates not from any specific action, like cheerleading, but from a basic belief in your ultimate mission in life and your ability to achieve it.

This means more than career success. Self-actualization is crucial to true happiness. But in order to actualize yourself, you need a mate with whom you can be yourself—someone with whom you can shed your public persona and feel comfortable being vulnerable.

One respondent describes her husband as her anchor. She depends on him for the support to just let her be herself. This is what I call "existential" support—someone who demonstrates faith in your innate goodness and capabilities.

She needed a partner who could contribute to her personal growth. As she says, "I just felt that I couldn't be all that I was without this partner." If she wants to go in a different direction in her career or her personal life, she knows she has a stable supporter.

> I think that's one of the reasons I chose him rather than all the other men I met in my life, because I felt that whatever I was was okay for him. He's one of the few people who accepted all the parts of me.

His acceptance allowed her to overcome many of the obstacles to her growth. His only demand is that she meet her own ultimate goals. She can set the time frame for meeting these objectives. She knows that he will be there no matter what.

A Partner During Difficult Transitions

Our greatest need for support comes during major life transitions, times when we must change careers, focus, lifestyle, or overall direction. During life passages, a supportive spouse can help us make a smooth transition and safe landing. Our mate may even be the catalyst spurring us on during these tumultuous periods.

Michael supported Susan when she wanted to change her status from freelance writer to corporate manager. He knew she had reached the point where she dreaded taking on another freelance assignment. When she was offered a full-time job as managing editor of a corporate newsletter, he encouraged her to take it, even though he knew that his life at home would change a good deal.

They asked themselves some hard questions about the effect of her transition on Michael. Would he suffer because of her new job? Would he have to cut back on his work hours to spend more time at home? They decided to make the leap for the overall good of their relationship, even though the transition would be difficult for both.

Tim likewise relied on his mate when he left his comfortable management job to start his own company:

> There's no question that without her support, her openness, not only her time commitment to the business, her more or less going along with what I was contending was a good financial move, the business would never have happened.

As you move through the life cycle, you often face incredibly difficult decisions—momentous life changes in career, geographical location, status. Without your mate's support, such transitions may prove insurmountable. You must hope that your mate supports you, and grows with you, as you move through life's challenges.

The Successercize that follows should help you gain a deeper understanding into your most important relationship.

How Supportive Is Your Mate?

In a way, you have probably been evaluating your mate as you read the preceding section. This Successercize will allow you to take a more systematic look at just how supportive your mate is.

1. Does your mate offer you guidance and advice on your career and life?   Y   N

2. Does your mate reflect well on you to your boss and colleagues?   Y   N

3. Does your mate cheer you on when you feel low?   Y   N

4. Is your mate genuinely happy for you when you succeed?   Y   N

5. When you do succeed, is your mate there to help you celebrate these achievements?   Y   N

6. Does your mate contribute to your self-esteem, generally making you feel good about yourself and your ability to meet your maximum achievements?   Y   N

7. During times of difficult career and life transitions, is your mate supportive of you?   Y   N

8. Does your mate take equal responsibility in the area of technical support, such as cleaning the house, balancing the budget, doing the laundry?   Y   N

9. If you have children, are you and your mate   Y   N
   equally responsible for getting the kids up in
   the morning, taking them to school, helping
   with their homework?

10. Is your mate an anchor in your life, always   Y   N
    there for you no matter what your goal?

The above questions should give you an insight into whether
your mate is providing the types of supports you need.

WHEN SABOTAGE BEGINS AT HOME

Although a supportive and cooperative mate is critical to career and life success, not all of us are lucky enough to have
such a spouse. In this section we will look at some of the
obstacles to support—the competition that emerges between
two upwardly mobile mates, the problems that arise when one
member lags behind the other, and other divisive elements of
a relationship.

Competition

At work, we compete for money, status, power, and promotions. For many organizations competition is the lifeblood of
company growth. But when mates compete with each other,
either consciously or unconsciously, each member of the couple moves from a supportive role to an adversarial one and
risks destroying the very basis of the relationship.

Living in a two-income family puts an enormous strain
on the interpersonal relationship between husband and wife.
One of the main sources of this strain is competition. Some
couples, instead of seeing both incomes as a source of a common pool, instead view them as an indication of superiority or
inferiority vis-à-vis each other. Once these comparisons begin,
they are hard to stop.

The situation of Nicole, a human-resources manager at a large accounting firm, typifies the many complexities of the competing-partners relationship. Nicole is married to a bonds trader who makes slightly less than she does. Very conscious of this disparity, her husband makes excuses for it, ranging from "You work in New York, I don't," to "Accounting firms pay more." He even attempts to disparage her accomplishments at the firm, telling her that "no one takes human resources seriously." This backbiting is a sure indication that they are already in the marital danger zone.

If he were to become the higher earner, their problems would probably remain. Several of Nicole's statements suggest that *she* would be jealous if her husband suddenly pulled ahead of her in the salary race. Clearly they need to sit down and discuss their individual goals and needs. They have to clarify, to themselves and to each other, how they feel about each other's success. After all, one partner is bound to make more money than the other.

In many marriages, the salary and occupational progress of one mate becomes a major consideration. It seems that the partnerships are based less on love than on the desire to buy a house or to gain an upper-middle-class standard of living. One executive I interviewed wonders what is down the line for these new "marriages of convenience": "God forbid if things ever get tight. If these people need some heavy support for each other, I just wonder what would happen."

Relationships thrive when each partner is interested in the other's success as a means to that person's happiness. Without such an attitude, the mate's achievements begin to appear as a threat.

When One Mate Lags

Another tension in relationships derives from a gap between the mate's two careers. Cynthia, for example, is dealing with a situation in which her husband's career is lagging significantly behind hers.

Both Cynthia and Dave work in high-tech engineering. Although she is advancing quickly, she describes him as being in a rut. Though frustrated from the restrictions his job puts on his creativity, he seems to lack the drive to change his situation. When they first met, he seemed ambitious. But now she is beginning to view him differently. She suspects that she herself may have inadvertently dampened his drive.

> Dave did well by marrying me. He doubled his income and his standard of living. He now has a house, three cars, a good life. He sees me getting ahead, and he's very comfortable. He'll stay home, take care of the kids, in a smoking jacket, and I'll be walking out with a briefcase.

This is not the marriage she wants—although some women do. For Cynthia, support means having someone who is her professional equal. From her point of view, if Dave is not her equal, he can't fulfill a role she desperately wants filled, that of constructive critic. She wants him to know what she's talking about when she discusses her job with him. They must have a common frame of reference. As she outdistances him in technical knowledge and career experience, Cynthia feels that Dave's ability to support her in this capacity is considerably diminished.

Dave is responding to his wife's successes with indifference, probably because he is threatened by her development. If your mate is threatened by your success, he or she may withdraw a variety of supports, including the willingness to celebrate your good fortune. In Cynthia's case, Dave's refusal to celebrate her accomplishments crushes her momentarily and renews her self-doubt. "His lack of enthusiasm for my progress plays into my own insecurity, that women shouldn't be engineers in the first place."

The Varying Reasons for Nonsupport

Spouses can withhold support in any number of ways and for any number of reasons. The permutations are endless. For instance, you may both be pursuing successful careers, and suddenly you are confronted with the need to move to another city for upward mobility. Will your spouse make the move for you? Will he or she agree to become one-half of a "commuter couple"? Will your spouse sacrifice his advancement for yours? Would you do it for his career?

Or let's say that one of you decides to change careers for personal fulfillment or inner satisfaction. You may want to terminate your stockbroker career and become a carpenter, an artist, a writer. Will your mate support your move, or withdraw the technical and ego supports so necessary for your success?

Sometimes one partner cannot or will not become part of the other's public persona. They won't play the corporate game, won't make the personal transformations necessary to enhance the other's personal image.

Regardless of the form that a mate's nonsupport takes, it is nothing to be treated lightly. Nonsupport by a lover or mate can wreak far more havoc on our ability to succeed than sabotage by jealous co-workers.

Unless your mate accepts your career and life goals, he or she will not give you the necessary ego supports that you so desperately need to achieve your goals. If you doubt how much you depend on such bolstering, think of how often you turn to your mate for confirmation that your last actions were the right ones. Think of how many times you check your mate's reactions to your career and job decisions before you act on them.

We become so dependent on our mate's approval that we don't even notice it—until that approval is withdrawn. And once the mate begins to withdraw approval, we suddenly lose subtle but vital ego supports that colleagues and bosses cannot supply. Once those esteem-building supports are gone, we may have problems accomplishing our goals.

The trick, then, is to develop a relationship in which each partner understands and accepts the other's goals, and works with the mate to achieve them.

If your mate is withdrawing support or is not offering it at all, take heart. In the next section we will talk about ways of avoiding some of these pitfalls and making your mate part of your supporting cast.

BUILDING A SUPPORTIVE RELATIONSHIP

By now you should have an understanding of the types of support your mate is providing. Successercize 6 should have sensitized you to the extent to which your mate is supportive. You should also have some insights into whether your mate is sabotaging you, or whether the seeds of the destruction of your relationship have been sown.

If your mate is not supporting you to the extent you consider necessary, you have three options: you can try to improve your mate, or leave the relationship, or—as so many people do—overlook reality. Hopefully you will decide to improve your situation by attempting to make your mate a supporter.

Your first consideration here is whether your mate has the ability to be a fully functioning member of your supporting cast. It is next to impossible to change someone in fundamental ways. If your mate is selfish, self-centered, or uncaring of your needs, or if he or she is demanding, irresponsible, and childish, you will be facing an uphill battle.

If your mate does have your interests and the interests of the relationship at heart, there are ways to make the relationship a more mutually supportive one, to ensure that both partners become more in sync with the other's needs.

Discuss Common Goals

You will never become part of each other's supporting casts without at least sitting down and spelling out what each expects out of life. You may find it helpful to go back to the Successercize in Chapter 1, "Goal Inventory." If your mate hasn't done so, have him or her fill out this short questionnaire too, and compare your answers. You may be surprised to find that you share the same goals, and only need to find ways to meet them.

Use your responses to probe some areas of your relationship. Does either of you want to make a career change? Would you be happier living somewhere else? Do you want to take time off from work? Do you want to start a family?

One couple developed a five-year plan for themselves, which they periodically review. The plans may change, but at least they have some specific life and career goals to which they can hold themselves and each other.

Become Your Mate's Supporter

A relationship works best when both partners know what the other wants and are willing to actively work toward helping the partner reach that goal.

At its most profound, marriage allows both persons to become co-supporters in this growth process. The power of a close interpersonal relationship like marriage is such that each partner has the power to help the other self-actualize, to become the best they can be.

Tim and his wife, Nancy, have developed a sense of cooperation under fire by running a business together. They have made each other's quest for success much easier. "If I was shouldering all the tough decisions alone," Tim says, "I would have a real problem. By discussing it, we get two perspectives. We make mutual decisions."

After five years of being in business together, they know each other's value. In fact, Tim feels working together has actually strengthened the marriage.

> Working together, day after day, we have something more than our friends have in their relationships. I think we have more in common, especially because of the business. We have learned to laugh at many of our problems.

The more you are willing to support your mate's goals, the more likely he or she is to help you meet yours. This is a point that will be elaborated on in Chapter 8, on becoming a member of another's supporting cast.

Turn Competition into Cooperation

As mentioned earlier, many couples find themselves in a competitive situation—for power, money, or esteem—a competition that threatens to turn supporters into saboteurs.

Both partners, if they are to build a supportive relationship, must guard against the effect of outside status, pressures, and stresses on the relationship.

Susan and Michael see themselves as partners, not competitors. Michael understands that for Susan, her salary buys a lot more than goods. Her earnings are an affirmation of her value, a perception Michael supports.

Competition between spouses is not without its touch of irony. Some people are so intent on minimizing the threat of competition from a mate that they marry someone several rungs below them in terms of intelligence, wit, and talent. While eliminating competition, they are also leaving themselves without someone who can advise them on their personal and career problems.

You have to make the choice. The more talented your spouse, the more potentially threatening. But the glue of any relationship comes from within, not from any objective conditions. The stronger the bond, the more each partner sees himself or herself as a member of the other's supporting cast, and the less the chance that competition will ever become an issue.

Ask for Support

What kind of support do you want and need? Perhaps there are certain roles, like esteem builder and catalyst, that you feel only your mate can fulfill.

If your mate is not fulfilling these roles, don't assume that he or she is unwilling to do so. You would be surprised at how often unsupportive spouses actually think they are fulfilling their roles just fine. They may not even be aware that they haven't given their mate a good pep talk in months. You may have to directly ask your mate to meet some of your needs.

Keep the Lines of Communication Open

The best-laid plans can go awry if people don't have time to communicate. You may both want to help each other, may want to learn each other's goals and hopes, but have a hard time keeping the lines of communication open. It is quite easy for members of a two-career couple to lose contact. Sometimes daily schedules make it almost impossible to touch base.

Here are some practical pointers for maintaining those lines of communication:

- Develop set times in the week or month when the two of you can specifically discuss where you are in your lives, what you want, how things have changed.
- Make sure you are really hearing what the other is saying. (More on listening skills will appear in the next chapter.)
- Make sure you leave time for daily contact. Many couples have set times to call each other at work during the day.

Some who work in the same city make an effort to occasionally have lunch together.

- If you have children, of course you spend your extra time
  with them. Try to make this a shared activity.

SELECTING A MATE FOR YOUR
SUPPORTING CAST

Up to this point we have assumed that you already have a
mate, or have lined up someone with whom you will spend
the rest of your life. However, if you are in the process of
evaluating a lover or fiancé in terms of his or her potential for
becoming a lifelong member of your supporting cast, you will
want to pay careful attention to this section.

In view of the current high divorce rate, perhaps many of
us are going about mate selection in the wrong way. Could it
be that we choose mates for all the wrong reasons? Could the
skyrocketing divorce rate in some way be caused by the fact
that partners don't understand each other's life and career
goals in the first place, and then fail to support those goals
when they become apparent?

If you are seeking a mate who will become a true member
of your supporting cast, you should factor into your search
some of the following criteria.

Choose someone who will support your career goals. Too
few couples during their dating phase sit down and discuss
how they want to live their lives. They may discuss what kind
of house they want to live in, but they don't always talk about
the type of career they want and how much time and energy
they want to devote to work.

Only by investigating these issues will you discover whether
your prospective mate is willing to share the household work-

load, to move if necessary, to put up with your longer hours during your career's formative years. If you are in your thirties or forties and are evaluating a prospective mate, you may have to present certain irreversible conditions of your life: you are an established attorney, for example, who must work 50 hours a week and travel one week a month.

I am always surprised that some people think they can hide the hard facts about their career requirements from their mates and then spring them on them after the wedding ceremony.

Choose someone who believes in you. At times in your career, the difference between making it and failing may be your mate's faith in you and your abilities. Many of the people I interviewed claim that at times their mates had even more faith in their ability to succeed than they had themselves. Their spouse's belief in them carried them through difficult times.

Look for someone who respects your field. In this age of specialization, no one can know everything about every occupation. But you should at least look for someone who is interested in your field and respects it. Remember, you will probably be discussing your work on a daily basis with this person. (Hopefully, you in turn will respect your mate's field of endeavor.)

Look for someone who can motivate you. Since the cheerleader role is so important, you need someone who can motivate you even in adversity. Your prospective mate should have a positive personality and be optimistic about life in general.

One of my respondents terminated her engagement to a law student when she discovered that he lacked any real interest in his chosen field. Although she was attracted to him, she ended the relationship because she thought his attitude toward work and life in general would adversely impact her own career growth. It looked as though he would do well monetarily (he was already clerking with a big-name law firm), but he did not display the ambition or dedication that she considered important.

> I wanted to share my life with somebody who is ener-gized and excited by what he's doing. Besides, somebody who wasn't going to be enthusiastic about his own work would probably have a hard time being enthusiastic about mine.

Current thinking suggests that you should seek a mate who "accepts you as you are." True, it may be comfortable to settle in with someone who is undemanding, who has no expectations of your achievements. But while this is a popular romantic image, it is more important to find someone who sets high standards for you in terms of goals and behavior.

Be wary of potential mates who are lethargic, nonchalant, directionless, and unenthusiastic. This type of person may be lenient with you when you fall short of your goals, because they themselves are weak. But it would be surprising if they are in any real sense excited about your career.

Look for someone who can effect positive change. You want someone who can change you for the better. Your spouse may have a better grasp of your overall ability and direction than you yourself have. One of the magical elements of close relationships is that each member often acts as a catalyst to the other, guiding him or her along the road to higher achievement.

Although this is a difficult characteristic to detect in a prospective mate, you might look for subtle indications. For instance, try to notice whether you have made positive self-improvements or achieved some new goal since you began dating this person.

Look for someone who can grow with you. One of the reasons mates (and others) may sabotage you is because they see you as a threat. As you outdistance them, you make them feel insecure. They react by withdrawing support for your career.

Look for someone with potential to grow as you grow. You should assess your mutual goals in much the same way that married couples should. Use the Successercize approach to explore your common values and your individual visions of the future.

What About Love?

You may feel that the above criteria seem to leave love out of the selection equation. You may rightly feel that while you need a mate who can help you succeed, it is equally important to find someone you love. Isn't love the crucial criterion in a relationship?

My response is an unqualified yes. The question, though, is this: Why would you fall in love with someone who is anything less than totally supportive? The "perfect" mate is someone who listens to your problems, provides emotional support, and is essentially noncompetitive with you. If you are in love with someone who violates these criteria—who competes with you, sabotages you, and withdraws support at crucial times—have you ever asked yourself why?

Perhaps you are replicating earlier lack of support from parents, teachers, and lovers. Perhaps you feel you deserve no better. Maybe, like millions of people, you think that love will solve all, that the nonsupportive mate will change. Sadly, this is seldom the case.

Seven Signals of the Supportive Partner

Are there subtle indicators that help you assess whether your future partner can meet the criteria we just discussed? Do

people emit signals which imply that they are essentially supportive, giving, and concerned about your future and career as
well as their own?

The following points should help you determine whether
your potential mate can function as a member of your
supporting cast. (Actually, these traits apply universally—to
friends, colleagues, and parents as well.) The supportive person:

Shows interest in you. You've just gotten engaged and
you're meeting your fiancé for dinner. You're bubbling with
excitement over the promotion you've just received, and you
begin to tell your prospective mate the news. If he is supportive he will listen, ask questions, and show interest.

However, if you find that he is more interested in discussing his new car; that for every five or ten minutes of conversation about you, you spend an hour discussing his problems;
that he cuts you off in mid-sentence—you can assume that this
person is fundamentally uninterested in you. Beware: this is a
pattern that probably won't change when you get married.

Understands your behavior. Only someone who is in tune
with your moods will be able to act as cheerleader, advisor,
esteem builder, public relations specialist, or celebrator. Your
prespective mate must understand why you do things and the
nature of your ambitions if the two of you are ever to discuss
what's really bothering·you.

Someone who is in touch with you can understand your
frame of reference. Your mate is then in a position to make
constructive comments about how to improve your situation.

Asks what you are doing. Does your prospective mate
seem to have the time to show concern for your problems?
The supportive mate will go out of his or her way to inquire
into your general progress.

However, if your partner never asks how your day has been going—if you always have to volunteer information or assertively take over the conversation—then the person is emitting signals of total self-centeredness and may be incapable of filling support roles for you.

Sees your success as his or her own. If you find that your partner is gratified when you do well, you have indications of long-term support. The best relationships are cloaked in an ambiance of "as you progress, our relationship gets stronger," and "we're in this together."

In the early stages of a relationship you can usually tell whether your prospective mate wants you to succeed. If you receive many positive comments and encouraging words for your activities and accomplishments, this person may already see himself or herself as part of your supporting cast.

Supports you in social situations. You can usually judge someone's potential support by their willingness to stand by you when you are verbally attacked or sabotaged. This might happen at parties, social gatherings, family get-togethers, or business meetings. You may be the butt of a joke or the object of a cutting remark about your looks, your job, your goals.

Watch how your mate reacts to these situations. If he or she backs away or gives lukewarm support, you may have an early indication that this person is unwilling or unable to help you when problems arise.

Remembers what you've said. People who care about you remember what you've told them—about your likes, dislikes, career problems, personal battles. If your mate regularly forgets facts that you have communicated, this is a sign that he or she may be tuning you out. Even though you may be receiving equal time in the conversation, it is evident that the other person isn't listening. The person who listens well is more prone to support you throughout your life.

Supports you during crises. Certain crises may come up during courtship that require the prospective mate's assistance—a death in the family, for example, or the loss of a job, or an accident. These incidents provide an acid test of a potential spouse's level of support and commitment. Those who are unresponsive in the early months of a relationship will not change during marriage. If anything, they may become more indifferent, more drawn into their own problems and less sensitive to the partner's.

During your "serious dating" period, be conscious of the extent to which your prospective mate is caring and sympathetic when crises arise. The person who isn't there for you during those periods will never become a true member of your supporting cast.

No marriage is perfect. The divorce rate is proof of that. But people are also remarrying in great numbers, which suggests that soon after divorce they realize that something is missing.

The best marriages are the ones in which both partners are really concerned about the other's success and ultimate happiness. You deserve to have a mate who helps you reach your highest level of achievement, and to whose well-being and growth you are equally committed.

CHAPTER EIGHT

Joining Another's Supporting Cast

A recent Harvard study of entrepreneurs revealed that while independent superachievers all possess the standard entrepreneurial qualities—ambition, perseverance, and a propensity to take risks—none acts completely independently. As has been suggested throughout this book, people become successful because they are able to gather around them other people to meet their needs. According to the Harvard report, the image of the entrepreneur as the lone wolf is a fallacy.

The question is, of course, how do superachievers gather this supporting cast? Most successful people know that you can't just ask for support and expect to receive it. If you want others to become part of your supporting cast, you must become part of theirs, by showing a readiness to help them attain their goals. You have to let potential supporters know, either overtly or by implication, that their support of you will bring benefit to them.

What does it mean to become part of another's supporting cast? Just being a friend, mate, or co-worker does not necessarily mean that you are part of a supportive circle. Becoming part of another's supporting cast implies a much more intensive concern for the needs and goals of others. It means making a commitment to their future, helping them reach their maximum potential.

Most supporting casts are characterized by synergy— people acting together for one another's betterment, helping where they can, asking for help where they need it. This synergy emerges only when everyone involved understands the benefits of mutual support.

Of course, regardless of your good intentions, your abilities and resources determine just how far you can go in supporting others. So you must carefully assess your own strengths to understand what your true capabilities are.

In this chapter you will learn how to discover others' needs and how to listen closely to what others are really saying about themselves. You will also get a chance to inventory your strengths to determine what resources you have to support others.

WHAT DO PEOPLE REALLY WANT?

Most high achievers I have interviewed suggest that the ability to identify others' needs is a requisite for success. One senior executive has come up with a little test to help his junior managers think through this problem of supporting others:

> I ask them to tell me how they would motivate a 40-year-old machinist whose job will not change, and who must continue working at the same level for the next 25 years. What should they "give" that person to motivate him to higher performance levels so that they can operate the plant correctly and efficiently?

His junior managers come up with any number of solutions. Some suggest paying this man more to get him to work harder. Others say they should assure him that he has a job for life. Many of the young managers think they could motivate the machinist by company recognition of his contributions through award ceremonies and fancier titles.

In a sense, there is no "right" answer to this question. The executive is trying to get the junior managers to envision this veteran's needs and to specify how they would go about fulfilling them—from our point of view, how they would become part of the machinist's supporting cast.

Whether in a work or personal situation, we all must face the challenge of determining others' needs. Certainly in a marital or parental relationship, this activity is critical to everyone's happiness. Although unraveling the complexity of even one person's needs may be a challenge, you will find this task easier if you recognize that all people are motivated by a combination of needs, such as power and material goods, in varying proportion.

Let's look at the specific needs that many people share.

Material Goods

Many people are motivated, in their lives and in their jobs, first and foremost by material needs—by money, and what it can bring them.

What kind of support would such a person want most from you? Probably he will be interested in any activity that will help him increase his earning capacity, including assistance in moving up the organizational ladder, starting a business, or making money on the stock market. On the job, you could do any number of the activities mentioned in Chapter 5 to help people who are motivated by material needs to reach their goals. You could assist them in writing proposals, help them develop ideas and get their ideas heard, show them off to the higher-ups, provide them with time off to take extra classes, or provide them with specific career guidelines. You could serve as contact, sponsor, or even financier to help people realize their material goals.

Power

Bob Allen, chairman of AT&T, realizes that people operate best when they are given power and authority. Recently Allen met with several middle managers who presented an interim report on a new product proposal. Although many CEOs believe they should make middle managers wait before giving final approval for such a proposal, Allen surprised these employees by giving the go-ahead without waiting for the final feasibility study. He listened to them present the facts, asked them a few questions and, as Allen tells it, "made a decision and 'turned them loose.' "

By empowering these people, Allen let them know he was part of their supporting cast. Not sensing people's need for power can lead to disaster. Frank, a senior manager, was offered the position of division president in a large drug firm. He was promised not only stock options and a substantial increase in salary but also the authority to run the division. This was the most important position he had ever held, and one he felt he was well suited for.

After three weeks he quit and returned to his old firm. Why? Because he quickly discovered that standing over him in his new job was a group president who actually set policy, made final product decisions, and determined the direction of all divisions. When it came down to it, Frank's role was to implement someone else's policies. This was not what he wanted.

Some people, like Frank, have a need not so much to acquire wealth and material goods but to exercise power—

over others, over things, over organizations—and would probably take a cut in pay to get a job with more power. They
might quit a job that gave them less authority, regardless of
the increase in salary. They are generally the leaders and
implementers.

Respect

Regardless of what other motivations compel them, most people have an innate need to be respected.

If you want to become a member of others' supporting
casts, you must begin to look past their roles—father, worker,
brother—and value people for their inherent worth. At work,
you must not regard people in terms of their functions—as
robots or machines that deliver to you some product or paper.
Instead you must treat them as human beings, people with
something to contribute. This lesson is lost on many managers
fresh out of business school, who seem to regard lower-
ranked workers as mere parts of the production process. Subordinates and staff are quick to sense a boss's or co-worker's
lack of respect. Rather than motivating people to win you over,
this attitude is a surefire way to invite sabotage.

It is possible to show respect even while criticizing or
disagreeing with someone. One middle manager describes a
situation in which her boss disagreed with her over how to
expand the work force and recruit new workers. Many bosses
would use this situation to flatten the worker's ego by pulling
rank and terminating the debate. Instead, she left his office
feeling like a truly valuable person.

Her boss knew how to disagree with her while still showing respect. He listened carefully to her criticism of his re-
cruitment plan, never becoming defensive, and then outlined
all the alternatives he had considered in coming to his conclusion, including some that she was now voicing to him. Just the
fact that he took the time to convince her of the rightness of

his position showed her that he respected her as a person. She walked out of the meeting feeling that, in spite of their momentary differences, he was her supporter.

Attention

Some people want more than your respect. They want some signal that you are aware of their existence, that they are on your mind. This is true on the job, in marriage, and in most other interpersonal situations.

Since many people are quick to infer that you are ignoring them, you must cater to people's need to receive attention. There are many ways to do this: send Christmas cards, thank-you notes, and presents; pay compliments; pick up the phone to say hello.

Informal one-on-one situations are the best places to demonstrate your willingness to pay attention. You must learn to focus on what people say and let them know you are really hearing their message. Later in this chapter we will deal with how you can improve your listening skills as a way of convincing others that you are really giving them and their message ample attention.

Recognition of Their Work

In much the same way that people need attention and respect, they also want others to believe that what they produce is worthwhile.

As we have seen, children need to have their accomplishments noticed. In our earlier discussion we saw how important it is that the parent show an interest in the child's work. As a result of this attention the child will feel that his talents, and hence himself, are appreciated.

In the work environment, you can become a supporter of both subordinates and superiors by recognizing the worthiness of their work. With subordinates, you need to compliment their accomplishments to show appreciation. In the case of superiors, you have to be more creative in paying homage to their work. Some feel that the best way to show superiors that you value their work is to assume the student role, actually asking them to "show me what you know." By asking superiors (or anyone, for that matter) to share their knowledge, you are showing that you value what they do.

One executive suggests saying something like, "I have done this much on my project, but I would like your feedback on it. Give me alternatives, let me learn from your wealth of experience." You are cueing the superior to the fact that you value his or her knowledge and accomplishments. As he puts it,

> I would feel flattered if someone came up to me and asked me to tell them how to do such and such. Just seeking me out shows that you have given some prior thought to the possibility that I am a valuable person.

Indeed, often the most important thing you can give a person is validation, affirmation that they possess useful, meaningful knowledge.

In the nonwork environment, be sensitive to those occasions when others are asking you implicitly for recognition. A friend may be working on a painting or refinishing a chair, entering a marathon or competing in a bike race. She may mention these activities to you in order to get a positive reaction, an emotional perk. Take advantage of this window of opportunity. In one moment you may be laying the groundwork for future support from this person.

Prestige

Some people are primarily motivated by prestige. This may translate into a job title, a large office, a big staff, or other status symbols.

This type of person is after the glory. He would even rather have a big office and fancy title than real power. Supervisors, subordinates, and friends of the prestige seeker have long since learned that to recruit this person into their supporting cast, they must help him in the quest for glory. If you want to be such a person's sponsor, you should be in a position in your company to see to it, for example, that his title is enhanced or his office enlarged.

Joining the supporting cast of such people can help you immensely. For instance, they may be able to deliver to you a wealth of social and business contacts as they move up. They may some day be able to involve you in some charmed circles from which you have previously been excluded.

Information

People need information—about jobs, other people, unpublicized events. The more you become part of people's information networks, the more you will be construed as a member of their supporting cast. By providing people information, you can bring them closer to their other goals, such as power and material goods.

Bosses consider you more loyal when you report back to them positive or negative information. If you get to the point where your boss can count on you as being "in the know" and can rely on you for counseling, you will shine as a supporter.

A Sense of Purpose

Another area that needs to be considered is people's need to have a sense of purpose, whether in their jobs or in daily life. For instance, many executives who believe in the innate worth of the corporation and its mission are purpose-driven: their ultimate personal mandate is to make the organization work. Naturally, if you want to attract their attention and get their support, you have to be aware of this need.

They will consider as part of their supporting cast anyone who helps them fulfill their sense of purpose. In turn you will be more likely to command support from the higher-ups if you are perceived to be meeting their corporate goals.

Security

Another factor that motivates people is the desire for long-term security. Many companies have noted that a certain percentage of employees work best when they feel assured they will have their jobs forever. This belief has become a central tenet of what is labeled the "Japanese" style of management.

If you were the supervisor of these people, you could start by letting them know that they can always stay with the company if they so desire, and that you will do whatever is necessary to help them keep their job.

In personal relationships, security is also a powerful core need. Friends need to know you will support them through thick and thin. Spouses—especially in today's divorce environment—need to feel that this marriage is "for keeps." Your marriage will work better if you amply reassure your mate that you are committed to the relationship, that you meant what you said at the alter, especially the part about "in sickness and in health."

A Sense of Belonging

Many people need to feel affiliated with a group that offers them acceptance. They need the company of others, as well as the sense of community that comes from being with a caring group of people.

As a supervisor, you would want to have such people work in an environment in which they could be part of a team. They would not be happy closed up in an office somewhere working alone at a computer terminal.

These people are often motivated by a need for acceptance. You improve your chances of becoming part of their supporting cast by interacting with them on a regular basis and showing them that you accept them for what they are.

The list of needs goes on. You should also be sensitive to others' need for independence, control, and self-expression. In fact, you can go back to the goal inventory in Successercize 1 to gain greater insight into what turns others on.

Of course, everyone has a combination of needs in varying proportions. To join someone's supporting cast, you may have to play a combination of roles. The main thing is that people sense that you want to help them achieve their ultimate goals, no matter what they are.

ASSESSING THE INDIVIDUAL'S NEEDS

There is no secret formula for finding out what others want and need. Everyone is unique. But here are some methods many people I interviewed have utilized successfully to determine what others—be they workers, superiors, or spouses—really want.

Respond to Their Requests for Help

Some people may simply ask for your support. They may say, "I have this problem . . . could you help me?" (Under some circumstances you can use this technique yourself to recruit members into your own supporting cast.)

Many people hesitate to ask for help, however. They may not really expect anyone to come through with any meaningful assistance. Given this fact, do not assume that because people do not voice their needs, they have none. In fact, they may be so overwhelmed by their problems that they don't even know where to start looking for help. Therefore, you may have to use a more direct approach.

Talk to Them

The direct method is usually the best way to find out what a person really wants. Often people welcome the chance to articulate their goals. In fact, showing you care enough to ask may be sufficient to put you in their supporting cast. Communication—between husband and wife, parent and child, superior and subordinate—is the key to the ability of two people to sense and meet each other's needs.

Surprisingly, many people hesitate to direct. Spouses sometimes are reluctant to probe too deeply into their mate's needs for fear of discovering that they won't be able to meet those needs. Bosses may not question subordinates, because they don't want to uncover any dissatisfaction they'd rather not deal with.

Subordinates may be so intimidated by powerful superiors that they fail to discover their needs. Are you intimidated by the thought of talking to those high up the organizational hierarchy to find out what they want, to go into their office and ask them their requirements on a project? If you are, then you will find it difficult to join a superior's supporting cast.

Granted, there may a big gap between you and a senior vice president. But for that very reason your input may be welcome. One middle manager makes it a practice to find out promptly from any new superior whether there are specific areas this boss wants him to focus on. He also tries to get a sense from the superior of how he wants to be communicated with: directly, through memos, informally, or at official meetings. The result is that he and his superior soon become a well-oiled management team.

People beneath you are similarly intimidated by *your* power, so they may not be quick to express what it is they really want from you.

When Bill, a senior vice president at Johnson & Johnson, was promoted to a division where his new staff knew him by reputation but not personally, he wisely assessed both the career and personal needs of each of his new staff members. He needed their support, but he also wanted to become a member of their supporting casts. To do this, he had to discover what each of them really needed. Assuming that his new subordinates wouldn't be forthcoming with this information, he decided to take the direct approach.

> I had twenty-some people working for me. I had a half-hour meeting with each, and found out who they were. I asked them about their families, their career needs.

He was especially interested in learning his new charges' special needs or special fears. What did they think of the organization? How did they feel about recent organizational changes and cutbacks?

He also wanted to know if his employees were willing to take on responsibility and risk, and whether they were ready to charge up a hill for the division if they had to. At the same time, he wanted them to feel confident that he was a man of commitment and loyalty. He wanted them to know he had a game plan and would go to bat for them when times got tough.

Bill's strategy points out that the more you show people that you support their ultimate goals, the more they will support you. Because he used the direct approach, his employees now feel that he honestly cares about their ideas and, more important, their long-term career progress.

It also shows how critical it is to develop good listening skills. Because Bill learned to develop a keen ear for people's needs, they were convinced that he really heard what they were saying.

Talk to People Who Know Them

In some situations, it may be difficult to determine people's needs. Perhaps you have only minimal contact with them because they are working outside the office, or you're having a hard time communicating with them on a more personal level. This does not mean that you must abandon hope of joining their supporting cast.

If you are not able to determine others' needs by merely asking them, try a more indirect approach: assess what people close to them feel are their needs. One executive claims that secretaries or assistants can tell you everything about a person, from his favorite restaurant to his preference in information-transfer techniques. He suggests that you approach the secretary and say something like, "I'm working with your boss. Can you tell me how he likes reports done, what kind of information he wants? Does he like everything on one piece of paper?"

The secretary can give you insights into his management style. Does he like to delegate? If the answer if yes, perhaps you should be on hand when he has a particular job to perform. Does he need information on morale, reactions to policies? He may not tell you, but his secretary will.

Since the secretary is likely to tell the boss that you have asked these questions, he will learn that you are interested in supporting him in his goal of getting his job done.

You should also try to talk to peers of people whose supporting casts you wish to join. Your own boss may have insight into the personality quirks and career needs of other colleagues.

Keep Your Eyes and Ears Open

Some people have a hard time verbalizing their needs. Therefore it's essential that you also rely on nonverbal cues by keeping your eyes and ears open. Listen to the grapevine; notice who spends time with whom.

One manager just "wanders around," as he puts it. He observes his workers while they accomplish their tasks, has lunch with them, watches them on their breaks. He uses his intuitive powers to determine what they need.

Put Yourself in Their Shoes

A most effective technique for determining others' needs involves the ability to empathize. Empathy means that you sense, from a combination of words, gestures, and body language, what the person really needs.

Put yourself in another's shoes. If you were he or she, what would you really want? Power? More interaction with others? A higher salary? A more challenging job? Everyone is different. Never assume that what you want and need is equally true for everyone around you.

You must discover their true priorities. The more you are willing to hear what people are really saying about themselves and their ambitions, the better position you will be in to meet their needs.

LISTENING WITH CARE

The art of listening is a crucial element in establishing and maintaining supporting casts. By listening closely to others, you will be able to understand them better, a crucial first step in meeting their needs.

Moreover, inattentiveness is seen by many as a lack of commitment. If the people with whom you are communicating assume that you just don't care enough to listen, they will not accept you into their supporting cast.

Why We Have Problems Listening to Others

Have you ever spoken to a person who seems to be looking over your head when you speak, who seems to be formulating his own ideas while you are expressing yours? While this person may indeed care about your thoughts, his manner convinces you that he is totally uninvolved. He may be merely demonstrating poor listening habits, but you imagine he is not interested in what you have to say. You quickly decide you do not want him as a supporter.

Listening is a skill you will need to master in order to establish a bond between you and the person you want to support. A variety of obstacles can impede our ability to hear what others are actually saying to us. For instance, market research has uncovered the fact that the brain has the ability to absorb more than four times the amount of information per minute that people normally throw at us when they speak. So we actually hear "quicker" than people can talk, which leads us to occasionally drift or daydream when people speak to us. It's not that we are not interested in what they are saying. It's just that the mind tends to drift when it is not sufficiently occupied.

Another problem interfering with the ability to listen fully is noise or distraction. The noise level in the average office from telephones and machinery may make it difficult for us to concentrate unless we are behind closed doors. "Internal" noise is also an impediment: a headache, emotional concerns, stress, or mental conversations with ourselves.

Unfortunately, the individual at the receiving end of our inattention will simply assume that we are distracted because we are bored with his or her message, not that our senses are being overwhelmed by factors over which we have little control.

Some Negative Listening Habits

In addition to having trouble concentrating, some of us have developed listening habits that actually undermine our ability to communicate.

One of the worst listening habits is faking attention. Even when we are not certain what a person actually said, we act polite, look directly at the speaker, make automatic nodding responses, and say "yes." The speaker can usually detect the lack of interest and may assume that the listener is dishonest and insincere.

Some people, even though they are attentive, miss the real message. They may listen only to the facts, not the meaning behind the words. As a researcher and a writer, I have trained myself to listen for the whole message: not just the direct statements, but the totality of words, gestures, feelings, and the overall consistency of messages from one moment to the next. The good listener must become aware of the speaker's hidden messages.

Another way to miss the message, and thereby convince the other person that you lack concern, is to engage in irrelevant interruptions. You should solicit clarification of anything you don't understand, but needless interruptions interfere with the speaker's ability to communicate with you.

Alternatively, you may be using the time while the other person is talking to formulate your own thoughts rather than listening to what the speaker has to say. This is not the best way to communicate.

Developing Good Listening Habits

Listening with care is more than a series of tricks and techniques. Listening is a science that can be learned and perfected.

Learn to maintain your attention. If you are getting bored, don't start using the techniques people commonly employ to fake attention, like raising eyebrows. The other person will see you as a fraud and will probably lose his train of thought to boot. Instead, try to concentrate on what the person is saying, and maintain eye contact. You might try paraphrasing what the speaker is saying. Asking the other person to elaborate is an excellent way of increasing your listening comprehension.

If your attention is waning because you are impatient with the gap between how fast you process thoughts and how slowly people usually speak, find ways to fill in these idle seconds. Instead of letting your mind wander, use that extra time to review what the other person just said, or to read his or her body language, or to think of what you feel about the speaker's words. It is also a perfect time to try to determine the real meaning behind the words.

Resist the temptation to do all the talking. You may be so enthusiastic about a subject that you don't give the other person a chance to respond. Or you assume you know what the person is saying when you really do not. You may have a tendency to finish the speaker's ideas for him. Someone who has trouble articulating will quickly acquiesce to your "help" on the subject. As a result, you never hear what is really on this person's mind.

You can overcome these bad habits by simply allowing the other person a chance to make his point. Instead of finishing his thoughts for him, or offering yours, simply ask leading questions to help him communicate. Be especially wary of dominating conversations with subordinates. They may let you do this, but what you think is conversation may seem to be pontification from their perspective.

Do not give the speaker the impression that you are judging him by his style or mannerisms. If the other person thinks you are becoming judgmental, he will tend to censor his information. Show the speaker that you are concerned about what he is trying to tell you. What are his needs, and how can you help fulfill them? That, not his manner of delivery, is the issue.

Be attentive to the nonverbal aspect of communication—body language. Much of what the speaker actually means comes through movement cues. A relaxed posture shows that the speaker is comfortable in what he is saying. But if the person seems to be moving away from you, he may want unconsciously to avoid the conversation. (There are any number of books on body language and its interpretation.)

So watch alertly for signals that convey other people's true feelings about you. The person who acts stiffly in your presence probably doesn't want you in his supporting cast. The chemistry is just not there, and he probably wouldn't exhibit the trust needed to be a member of your supporting cast.

Always keep in mind *why* you are communicating with others in the first place. You not only want to hear what they are saying but also want to understand their ultimate needs. Some people want criticism, some want a chance to sound off, some want help in developing their ideas, some want approval.

You should use the "listening with care" approach as a way to detect other people's needs and as a way of making them feel special. Listening properly is one of the greatest gifts you can give, and a sure sign that you are a useful supporter.

WHAT DO YOU HAVE TO OFFER?

By now you have a good idea of how to determine the kind of support other people need in a variety of areas. The next question is whether you have the capacity to meet any or all of those needs. Can you play the cheerleader or celebrator role in someone else's supporting cast? Do you have the ability to build other people's esteem, to fortify their self-image? What strengths do you bring to the table to help other people maximize their potential?

It's hard to be objective about yourself, but until you are honest with yourself regarding your capabilities, you won't be able to function as a true contributor to another's supporting cast.

There are two categories of capabilities, which can be labeled *personal* and *positional.* Successercize 7 in this section should help you inventory your strengths more systematically to give you insight into how you can specifically support others in achieving their goals.

Personal Strengths

Each of us possesses certain innate characteristics that we can use to help others. These traits may include native intelligence, the ability to think analytically, communicate with others, be creative, or form alliances. Physical characteristics, such as manual dexterity and personal attractiveness, fall into this category. Each of these assets allows us to play a variety of support roles for others, including advisor, sponsor, and catalyst.

What are your personal strengths? In what areas have you excelled throughout your life? Are you bursting with innovative ideas? Great at organizing others?

We don't always have a clear sense of the ways in which we can contribute to others' growth. A novelist I know is dating a woman whom he considers his catalyst. The combination of her high-spirited personality and intelligence provides the spark necessary for him to do superior work. Early in their relationship, however, this girlfriend was unaware that she played this catalyst role. When he revealed to her how important she was to his artistic growth, she gained new insight into her own value as a human being. She was then able to make an even greater contribution to his work, both as critic and catalyst. She realizes now that when she is in his company during his "moments of genius," she isn't in the way. In fact, quite the opposite—their discussions, heated arguments, even their physical relationship, energize and revitalize his creative powers.

Positional Powers

Sometimes our mere position in a structure makes us de facto candidates for others' supporting casts. In the family setting, for instance, older siblings are often surprised at the extent to which their position in the family structure automatically makes them role models for younger brothers and sisters. At work, every position offers a unique opportunity to contribute to others' growth. Subordinates can support their boss; supervisors can assist their underlings.

Often you can use the combination of your personal traits and position or job to facilitate others' quests for success. Let's take a quick inventory of your strengths through the following Successercize.

Assessing Your Ability to Help Others

This Successercize is aimed at helping you assess your ability to support others. Answer "yes" or "no" to each of these questions.

1. Do you have the kind of personality that allows you to make others feel good when they are down, to cheer them on during their rough periods?   Y   N

2. Are you able to connect people who are seeking jobs, or entry into organizations, with others who can help them?   Y   N

3. Can you loan people money when they require it, and offer them financial counseling when the need arises?   Y   N

4. Does your position in your organization give you the opportunity to sponsor others, shape their future, and promote them?   Y   N

5. Do you have the ability to perform positive "public relations" for people, telling others about their good qualities and accomplishments?   Y   N

6. Are you someone to whom others—in your social circle and where you work—look up to as a role model?   Y   N

7. Do you have the time and energy to act as a   Y N
   technical supporter for others?

8. Can you offer people constructive criticism   Y N
   when they need it?

9. Are you able to build people's self-esteem   Y N
   and encourage them to develop a positive
   self-image?

10. Do you provide those around you with the   Y N
    necessary spark, the energy they need to go
    forward and think in new directions?

11. When people in your life do well, do you cele- Y N
    brate with them their victories and accom-
    plishments?

12. Do you have the necessary knowledge and   Y N
    information to serve as an advisor to friends
    and colleagues?

The more questions you answered "yes," the more roles you
can play in others' lives. This assessment should also suggest
what roles you could play with a little more self-development.

USE YOUR STRENGTHS TO MAKE
YOURSELF VALUABLE

Having inventoried your strengths, you should next try to use
them in supportive roles.

Take, for example, a fairly common type of positional
strength: access to information. As part of your role in an
organization, you probably have some type of information to
share. That information, no matter how routine it seems from
your perspective, could probably be of benefit to someone
else. You can use it to help others whose supporting cast you
wish to join.

Because upwardly mobile people know that information is one of the commodities they can share with others, they have mastered the skill of gathering and dispensing this precious source of power. One young engineer, for example, used her knowledge and intelligence to become a highly valued member of her boss's supporting cast. Her boss, an organic chemist, headed several projects that required engineering expertise, a skill he sorely lacked. She realized early on that she had the knowledge necessary to make his projects successful.

She managed to make him aware of how her strengths complemented his knowledge and expertise, and he became convinced that she could help him succeed in his job. Eventually he would make no important move without her help.

> My boss increasingly looked at me like a team player. He was trying to make a useful contribution to the company. Since it had to be done from both an engineering and organic framework, the results of our working together have made him look good.

Because of her excellent work, her boss began to act as her public relations specialist, building up her reputation throughout the organization. He managed to get her an "exceptional" rating at her next performance appraisal.

Her story is a good example of how to capitalize on strengths that emanate from your particular position in an organization or a relationship. She understood that even as a subordinate, her position had a built-in power, rooted not in the organizational chart but in the knowledge she brought to her job. She realized that the best way to become part of her superior's supporting cast was to help him advance his career, which in turn enhanced hers.

People who can correctly assess their power in an organization and their personal strength are best prepared to use these strengths to help others achieve their goals.

DO YOU HOLD BACK SUPPORT?

Being able to fulfill roles and being willing to do so are two separate issues. Some people still hesitate to become members of others' supporting casts in spite of their ability to do so.

The reasons for this are many. Some people are quite simply threatened by the success of others, and therefore unconsciously withhold support. These people are trapped by their own insecurities, and thus they never acquire "people-developing" skills, because to them every recipient of support and assistance is a potential competitor.

Others withhold support because they are self-centered. They may have been so deprived of recognition early in life that they cannot even conceive of situations in which others' needs should take center stage. They also find it difficult to give compliments, as though giving recognition to another will rob them of the spotlight they so fervently desire.

Sometimes we withhold support from others because they remind us, perhaps subconsciously, of negative figures in our past.

If you find that such personal prejudices or irrational tendencies are preventing you from supporting others, you should seriously consider changing these behaviors and attitudes. If you don't, you will always be an outsider, removed from the basic cooperative relationships that help people succeed. You will be stifling your own growth.

The best technique to change the tendency to withhold support is to start taking quick dips in the lifestream of mutually supportive relationships. You could, for instance, make an effort to involve yourself in one mutually supportive relationship. Or you could try to fill one of the empty niches in someone else's supporting cast. You could also try to improve your listening habits as suggested above. You may then be able for the first time to really hear what people are saying about themselves, and you may gain a healthy insight into their needs.

If you find you are having real problems establishing interpersonal support relationships, the next chapter should prove particularly helpful. Are you afraid to enter supportive relationships? Shy? Introverted? Mistrustful? Chapter 9 will show you how to use a more structured support group to help ease you into developing a supporting cast.

MOST SUPPORT IS MUTUALLY BENEFICIAL

People who take an active interest in others' development often discover a serendipitous benefit. They themselves begin to grow—in knowledge, power, self-confidence, and self-esteem.

The first benefit to you is that you will quite simply feel better helping others. Speak to any successful teacher or parent and you will discover the warm feeling that comes when you contribute to another's future.

Second, the interaction between you and the person you are supporting becomes a learning process for both of you. Mentors learn as much from their protégés as the younger followers learn from them.

In addition, once you start to support others, your reputation as a "people developer" begins to spread. In an organization this can benefit your career immensely. I have seen numerous managers able to attract the "best and the brightest" because they have become known throughout the company as someone who can serve as a sponsor, catalyst, cheerleader, and public relations specialist for other employees. Attracting the best increases your ability to manage well and move up the company hierarchy.

Support, then, is a synergistic process. As you support others, you too begin to grow, personally and professionally. As you help others reach their maximum potential, you are more able to reach yours.

CHAPTER NINE

The Expanding Universe of Formal Supports

Most members of your supporting cast will be recruited from people in your social circle or those you meet on the job. You may have certain needs, however, that can be served more effectively by tapping formal supports or professional resources, including some services for which fees are charged.

There has been tremendous growth of formalized supports linked to organizations, corporations, private foundations, and other institutions. The areas in which you can receive formal supports are endless. There are agencies to help you bring up your children, plan your finances, organize your life, reduce stress, become healthier, and conquer your addictions. You should not hesitate to use these programs to enhance your life and help you achieve happiness and success.

There was a time—not all that long ago—when the stable nuclear family and the multigenerational extended family provided the individual with a number of services, especially in the area of child care. People could rely on family, church, and community to provide them with many supports—moral sustenance, inspiration, spiritual guidance, even financial assistance and counsel. But the individual in modern society is increasingly isolated from these institutions.

As the traditional sources of help have lost their effectiveness, however, other forms of support have sprung up to assist the individual. It's important that you become familiar with the expanding range of formal supports.

These technical supports can fill or supplement roles that are not being adequately performed within your personal supporting cast. These roles can include anything from a trained therapist to help you with your emotional problems, to household help with cooking and cleaning.

FORMAL MOTIVATORS

Do you feel that the people in your social circle or at work provide you with enough encouragement to achieve your goals? Do you feel that your co-workers, your mate, and your friends provide enough of the cheerleader role when you feel low? Are there people around for you when you want to celebrate victory? If your answer to these questions is no, then you may lack the support necessary to regularly motivate you to reach your maximum potential.

If you want this kind of support, there are several formal programs to help. The Dale Carnegie course is perhaps the best-known program to help in improving self-confidence, overall presentation of self, and public-speaking skills. Its longevity is testimony to its effectiveness. Toastmasters is a nationally recognized organization that builds people's self-confidence to speak in front of others.

Programs have evolved over the years to encompass a wide array of motivation techniques. Est and similar groups that blossomed during the late sixties and early seventies helped people develop the self-confidence necessary to reach their potential. Careertrac, a nationwide operation, provides

training in office politics, aggressiveness, and impression management. Many of these courses are aimed at women.

The most effective motivational programs are the ones
that help the participants understand why they haven't been
able to achieve their goals—what personal or professional
obstacles stand in their way. One motivational program in the
New York metropolitan area uses a combination of emotional
support and practical suggestions to increase self-image and
motivation. People enter the program in search of support to
attain a specific goal—to finish a dissertation, for example, or
start a business, or get a divorce. The program treats all goals,
and their obstacles, in much the same way.

Participants attend a series of three-hour group sessions
led by a trained moderator. Each person states the goal he
wants to attain and develops a detailed written plan for achieving the goal. He must reveal the action plan to the group, and
in subsequent sessions he must report to the group his progress, or lack of it, in reaching the goal. The group confronts
those who fail to act and encourages and rewards those who
work toward reaching their goal. Needless to say, procrastina-
tion is not tolerated.

One nationally franchised motivational program, Self-Talk,
uses the seminar method, but with a twist. Those who complete the six-session program are provided with audio tapes
offering confidence- and esteem-building messages to play
whenever the will to achieve success wanes.

You may want to consider these types of group supports if
your informal support network, or parental background, has
not provided you with good motivational mechanisms.

There is even a motivational program for children. The
Power of Positive Students (POPS), funded and operated by
Norman Vincent Peale's foundation, helps grade-school children improve their self-image and self-confidence. The program came into existence because it was felt that parents
today are too overburdened by work and career to fully play
their traditional role in these areas. The program utilizes a

series of videotapes that show children how to establish and accomplish realistic goals, deal with disappointment, and build their sense of self-esteem.

EMOTIONAL HELP WHEN YOU NEED IT

Sometimes we need more than motivational, informational, or goal-oriented support. We need a deeper type of assistance with personal problems or emotional concerns that either cannot or should not be addressed by members of our immediate supporting cast.

Therapy

If your problems seem too overwhelming or complex for anyone in your supporting cast to help you with, seek professional assistance. The right therapist, analyst, or mental-health professional will actually become a valued member of your supporting cast.

A good therapist can help you sort out personal conflicts, problems with office politics, and help you build or rebuild your self-esteem. He or she can serve the cheerleader, advisor, and celebrator role. Your therapist can even serve as an intermediary between you and your mate to help each of you become a member of the other's supporting cast. Since the therapist is not part of your home or work life, he or she provide an objective, outside perspective on your problems.

Addiction Treatment

On the current sociological landscape, one type of personal problem seems to outstrip all others: addiction. This malady, besides wrecking your personal relationships and your mental health, can quickly undo your career.

In order to be really successful, you must master yourself, which means controlling your compulsions. If you are addicted to food, drugs, or alcohol, there are a number of formal rehabilitation programs to help you overcome your problem and get on with your life.

Alcoholics Anonymous is one of the most successful support systems for helping people overcome their craving for liquor. Out of the AA model have come other programs to help conquer addictions, including Overeaters Anonymous and Gamblers Anonymous. The Weight Watchers organization, and the myriad of diet-conscious groups it has spawned, can help you overcome compulsions to overeat by helping you develop a lifelong diet you can live with.

A variety of treatment centers have arisen to help people overcome their need for drugs. Some are inpatient centers, such as Odyssey House, Daytop Village, and Synanon in California. Two of the more well-known are the Areba-Carial Institute and the Betty Ford Clinic, both known for treating the rich and famous. There is even a chain operation, Comprehensive Care, in Southern California. Some outpatient centers feature weekly group sessions, detoxification, and other valuable programs.

The examples of self-help groups are endless: crime victims' families groups, battered women's help groups, the hospice movement, AIDS victims organizations, and many others. All stand as testimony to the altruistic drive in our society. There is even an organization to help divorced individuals. Started in 1987 in Los Angeles, Divorced Anonymous includes people from all areas of life: teenagers, retirees, people married one year, people married 40 years. Although the organization's membership is 85 percent female, it helps both sexes recover from the emotional ordeal of divorce.

Functioning along the lines of Alcoholics Anonymous, the organization encourages the participants to heal one another. Since all members are at different points of the post-divorce experience, the newly divorced can learn from the more experienced divorcees how to deal with the pain of separation, their new economic status, job hunting, and a plethora of other problems. The members help one another take their minds off their own problems and boost one another's self-esteem. Real friendships develop.

With such a variety of programs available, you should not hesitate to seek emotional help when you need it.

HELP IN CHILD CARE

In the United States, over half of the mothers of toddlers, and most of the fathers, are employed. If you have young children and a job, you probably need child care during the day.

Some working people utilize a sitter in their home, while others drop off their children at a neighbor's or relative's house. A third alternative to which parents are turning to in increasing numbers is day care. Some day-care facilities, like Kindercare, are nationwide franchise operations. The demand for such care is reflected in waiting lists of a year or more for the better-known and dependable facilities. In addition to private day-care services, many state, federal, and local governments—as well as some companies—have assumed the child-care role to help parents balance work and home duties.

Regardless of the agency or organization you choose, there are several issues you must be concerned about.

- The day-care facility's hours must fit your schedule.

- You must be confident that the institution's personnel are trained in child care. Look into the center's licensing and screening procedures.

- If you want the center to be a true member of the supporting cast of you and your child, make sure that it can literally play the role of educator. Many have become real learning centers. Some even feature rudimentary computer training.

- You should decide what role you feel the center should play in your child's socialization. Do you want the center to teach your child values, norms, discipline, and rules of behavior? If so, interview the teachers, supervisors, and workers to determine what values they would like to impart to the child.

- The facility must be concerned over your child's safety. Centers vary greatly in the extent to which they ensure children's physical safety. Even though all child-care centers should meet some minimum state safety requirements, check this out yourself.

You must choose child care with your support needs, and those of your children, in mind. Child care can be expensive. And it doesn't leave you as free and clear of responsibilities as you might think. Most day-care centers will not accept a sick child, so an illness means that you or your mate will probably have to stay home to care for the child.

OTHER TECHNICAL SUPPORTS

You may be too busy to do many of life's more routine activities yourself. If you are single and living alone, or part of a two-earner family, you may have problems finding the time to cook, clean, fix your car, do your taxes, or repair your house.

Fortunately, you need look no further than the classified ads section of your local newspaper or magazines to find technical supporters willing to perform these tasks for a fee. The personal services field has proliferated in recent years, offering companies and individuals that will do everything from house-sit while you are on vacation to wait in line to register your car.

CORPORATIONS HELPING OUT

Corporations are joining the expanding world of formal support systems by establishing programs to help employees meet many of their needs. Companies are taking a more active interest in their employees' overall well-being, offering assistance in dealing with such issues as stress, child rearing, and financial management.

These programs should not be used as a substitute for a personalized supporting cast, but you should definitely consider corporate-based programs a bona fide addition to other support mechanisms.

Stress Management

Modern job situations are stressful. According to a recent survey in the *Wall Street Journal*, 1988 saw a dramatic jump in the number of job-related mental disability claims, caused in great part by the hectic nature of today's work and the aftershocks of major corporate downsizing.

Companies today are concerned with the negative impact of job stress on absenteeism, productivity, and turnover. Thus they have come to realize that it is in their own best interest to deal with employee stress directly.

If you suffer from stress, consider enrolling in any stress-management program your company provides. These courses, which many companies offer free of charge, show the individual how to deal with stress in his or her own way. Texas Instruments brings in consultants to teach employees a variety of coping skills and relaxation techniques. At John Hancock, employees learn to reduce stress through deep-breathing exercises. The Coors Company shows its workers how to deal with the stress of child rearing.

Some companies provide on-site therapy for those who feel overwhelmed by job stress. If you feel this need, you are not alone. One company thought that its newly hired "stress manager," a clinical psychologist, would receive a few inquiries and establish a manageable patient caseload when they announced his availability. They were shocked when 30 percent of the employees signed up for this cost-free therapy!

Some company's medical plans will pay, at least in part, for regular visits to a psychologist or social caseworker. Find out whether your employer is willing to go that extra mile to support your emotional well-being.

Nutrition and Health

Because of stress-related illnesses and early heart attacks among their employees, companies have become more concerned about their workers' health. They have responded to what they consider a major health problem by making available to their employees a plethora of programs to promote nutritional well-being and physical fitness. Many large companies, including Johnson & Johnson, Union Carbide, and Hoechst-Celanese, have adopted comprehensive wellness programs that help employees with controlling weight, stopping smoking, improving nutrition, and enhancing general health.

Day Care

Some corporations are expanding their support for the employee into the area of child care. The types of support vary widely.

Information and referral. At the very least, your company's human-resources department may provide information on local day care to help you in your search for the best-run and most cost-effective center. According to some analyses, close to a thousand companies in the United States, including giants like IBM, offer such information and referral services.

On-site day care. If your company operates an on-site day-care center, consider yourself lucky. Fewer than 300 companies in the United States operate such centers, among them Hoffman-LaRoche, Merck, Campell's Soup, Tandy, and Stride-Rite.

The benefits for employees are enormous. For one thing, the children are nearby during the work day, and many people feel more secure about day-care centers operated by their own employers. Equally important is the ease of dropping children off in the morning and picking them up at night near the workplace.

Employee voucher reimbursements. Some companies offer programs to offset child-care expenses, either by issuing the parent a voucher covering day-care payments or by compensating the day-care center directly. Companies that have this type of program include Polaroid and the Ford Foundation.

Funding of existing community programs. Other companies donate money to local independent day-care facilities. The centers may then give employees a discount or rebate for services rendered.

Salary reduction plans. One of the more convenient forms of child-care support is the salary reduction plan. In this program, the company reduces an employee's salary by the amount of the cost of day care. That money is then used to pay the day-care provider. This method can save the employee money in taxes, since the gross salary is reduced by the day-care payment. In most cases the company usually allows the employee to choose the child-care facility.

Financial Advice

In the most basic sense, the company is the employee's financier. However, many companies are more than willing to extend their services as financial analyst to help workers achieve financial stability for themselves and their heirs.

Some companies supply employees with accounting services to help them in such areas as tax-return preparation, tax shelters, and deferred investments. Some provide advice on long-range financial planning. Such a program might include hints on how to develop a portfolio of stocks and bonds, how to use real estate as a long-term investment, and how to plan for retirement through IRAs and other strategies.

Some companies will send employees to seminars on financial matters ranging from tax shelters to financing a child's college education. Some companies hold free seminars on financial matters on-site.

FORMAL MENTOR PROGRAMS— A NEW KIND OF SUPPORT

A new support phenomenon is emerging. Corporations, schools, and communities are looking at improved methods of providing support to newer recruits, students, and junior members. They are doing this through formal mentor programs, in which the organization actually links newcomers with senior persons who can guide, assist, advise, and sponsor them.

Why a Mentor Program?

The first formal mentor program I know of was developed about ten years ago by the Jewel Tea Company. Since then, numerous corporations have adopted formal mentoring programs, including Hoechst-Celanese, Federal Express, Pacific Telesis, Motorola, AT&T, Indiana Bell, and Johnson & Johnson. Recently, the formal mentor movement has spread from the corporate world to other fields. Hospitals are using mentor programs to provide nurses with psychological and technical support. Police departments are also furnishing mentors to rookies on the force.

As a consultant I have helped establish many mentor programs in corporations. The corporations receive several benefits. By supplying employees with mentors, the companies anchor them more securely into the organization, thereby reducing turnover. Formal mentoring is of particular significance to women and minorities, who traditionally have had a hard time cracking the old-boy network. Company-sponsored mentor programs also forge links between older male executives and lower-level minorities to enhance their movement up the organizational ladder.

Research is demonstrating the powerful effects of this new support system in education. Studies indicate that children's ability to read and write increases dramatically when they are assigned a mentor to oversee their literacy training. HOSTS, a West Coast organization that develops mentor programs for low-literacy youths, claims that mentors have been able to upgrade the reading skills of youths the school system considered unteachable.

The mentoring movement has come a long way. A few umbrella organizations have emerged to help accelerate the adoption of quality programs in a variety of fields. For instance, the International Mentoring Association, located in the Midwest, was formed to serve as a vehicle for practitioners and researchers to swap views and exchange information on mentoring, as well as to provide training to those who may want to set up formal programs. The newly created Uncommon Individual Foundation in Radnor, Pennsylvania, has sponsored the formation of the International Mentoring Center to serve as a research and referral base for formal mentor programs in both the corporate and nonprofit areas.

If your company or organization has a mentor program, avail yourself of this opportunity. A formal mentor program can help you build your support network quickly in a new organization, supplying you with a senior supporter who can help you develop your talents and who can show you the organizational ropes. This link with a senior mentor should help you achieve greater visibility in your organization.

If your company does not have formalized mentoring and you feel that because you are isolated from power you could benefit from such a program, suggest to your company's human-resources department that it start one. Many such programs have been initiated at the request of lower-level employees, often women and minorities.

Now that we've looked at a variety of formal support services available, think about which ones could be of greatest benefit to you. The following Successercize will help give you a clearer idea.

What Formal Supports
Do You Need?

The following questions should help you determine what types of outside formal supports you need to reach your maximum potential and your lifetime goals.

1. Do you feel you need more encouragement than the people around you can provide? Y N

2. Do you feel you need more cheerleading than people at work, your mate, and your friends can give you? Y N

3. Do you need outside help with cooking and cleaning? Y N

4. Do you need emotional support that doesn't seem forthcoming from friends and your mate? Y N

5. Are you unable to cope with addictions to drugs, alcohol, gambling, or food? Y N

6. Do you feel that you need outside help in remaining physically fit and nutritionally sound? Y N

7. Do you need outside agencies or individuals to help you plan your economic future, do your taxes, handle your finances? Y N

8. Do you have trouble making contacts and developing relationships through everyday interpersonal interaction? Y N

9. Do you need advice on your life and your ca-   Y   N
   reer that can't be provided by those in your
   social and work circle?

The more "yes" answers you gave, the more likely it is that
you should be seeking more formal supports.

THE ELECTRONIC FAMILY

Through the miracle of electronics, your support system can
now expand beyond the relationships you have established in
your job and personal life.

The Computer Universe

If you have a computer and a device known as a modem,
which allows you to connect your computer to a telephone,
you can expand your supporting cast geometrically. You can
set yourself up to contact any number of people, data bases,
and electronic services that can make a significant supportive
contribution to your life.

At first glance, the concept of technology as a member of
your supporting cast may seem unusual. But the modem can
help your computer connect to such worldwide electronic
networks as Compuserve, Genie, and the Source, which make
available information, people, and organizations.

Computer career services. Computer services allow you
to get your hands on available job descriptions from a variety
of companies and to share your résumé through the computer
with employers in your field. Any computer networking hand-
book should give you the names of services currently operating that allow you to enter information about yourself
and have it electronically passed on to hundreds of employers.

Computerized cast-building. The computer can help you develop your supporting cast. Through the networking services of some of the on-line systems mentioned above, you can meet prospective friends, business partners, or mates. Through the ever-expanding nationwide electronic family, you can discuss problems, get advice, or float an idea for a new business.

Financial data. Technology as a democratizing influence is nowhere more profound than in the area of finance. On-line technology has made it possible for the average individual to obtain detailed and sophisticated financial information. The computer has made it simpler and faster to access information on any number of companies that are willing to share their stock portfolios and profit reports with hungry investors.

You may not need a broker's advice anymore, what with such services as the Dow Jones News Retrieval Service, which will electronically reproduce and print the full status and history of any company you choose. There are both subscription and on-line fees for such service, but many investors feel it is well worth it.

General information. Need to know something about astrophysics, education, or social science? Do you need information on travel, computers, current events? The quickest way to acquire information is through computerized data bases. In addition to the vast array of information available on-line, most computer services offer access to Special Interest Groups, or SIGs, which meet in "roundtables" at set times to exchange information and give advice. In effect, computer networks provide the user an instant board of advisors. Previously, it would have taken months, and much expense, to gather together experts and aficionados in one room to discuss, analyze, and dispense information on a particular topic. Now this process can occur weekly at the push of a button.

The computer can also connect you with providers of other services, from accountants to house cleaners, mechanics, and babysitters, with whom you can be in immediate touch.

Reach Out and Support Someone

The telephone industry seems to show an honest desire to become part of the national formal support system. A wide range of exchanges, such as 976 and 540, and the 900 area-code number, can be utilized to link up with a variety of networks.

You can call a 976 exchange, for example, to hear your horoscope, pick a lottery number, or get advice on any number of issues. Over the last two years, the 900 exchange has dramatically broadened human contact. These numbers use the new advances in telecommunications technology to link people by phone in ways that would have been inconceivable just a few years ago. You probably have seen advertisements for these numbers. These telecommunications breakthroughs can help you broaden your supporting cast of cheerleaders and celebrators.

The fax machine phone lines connect you to others in an even more personal way. You can now utilize these machines to send text or pictures over the standard telephone system to someone at another fax machine at the other end. The device holds the possibility of revolutionizing many areas of cast-building behavior. In the dating area, for instance, you can now send your picture and bio to a prospective mate, and receive similar information in return, before the two of you ever meet.

The Mass Media

Want to know how to buy and sell real estate, get a job, bring up your children, find a lover, divorce a mate? The mass media is there to help you!

Television, radio, books, and videotapes have become part of the formalized support system, providing guidance and information—some of it superficial, but some of it sound—to millions of Americans on a regular basis. Whether it means watching "60 Minutes" on TV or listening to radio psychiatrist David Viscott, following a series on educational TV or reading a self-help book on financial strategy, the mass media can fill in many areas of your supporting cast.

In an ever more complex world, we want to know what other people think and feel, and we need to learn how they solve problems. We can get a full education on politics and sociology by listening to the plethora of guests on television talk programs such as Phil Donahue's, Oprah Winfrey's, and Geraldo Rivera's. A host of syndicated shows, such as "Home" and "Hour Magazine," bring into our lives the kind of information that was not shared with earlier generations. The explosion of "reality TV" demonstrates our great need for insights into how the world works.

Taken as a whole, the range of formal support systems, from corporate-sponsored day care to computerized dating, means that there are few limits to the people and organizations you can utilize to reach your maximum potential. You do not have to depend entirely on your immediate social circle, family, and business colleagues to achieve your goals.

Our society seems to be evolving into two categories of people: those "in the know" who gain access to the variety of services we have mentioned, and those scratching their heads wondering how the "insiders" do it.

You must unlock the door to this expanding world of formal supports, and one key to that lock is information. You must discover what services exist to fill in your support network and learn how to locate these services. Once you find them, you must aggressively pursue them. You must *buy* the book, *watch* the program, *question* your human-resources department, *connect* your computer.

The important message is that our world is being re-structured in such a way that although the family unit is changing, the neighborhood disappearing, and the old supports seemingly waning, other structures are replacing them. You just have to locate these new structures. Once you consider the world of formal structures a regular part of your supporting cast, you will know that you never have to be alone again.

CHAPTER TEN

The Post-Success Dilemma and Its Solutions

Imagine that the day has come when you have achieved many of the goals you set out to accomplish. You have done this by enlisting others' support to reach this goal, and in the process you have contributed to their growth. Believe it or not, there are some who think that when they reach this point—whether in their career or personal life—they no longer need supporters. "After all," they reason, "as my power and position increase, I should need the help of others to a lesser degree."

Of course, they are wrong! Support becomes *more* important as you proceed to climb upward. In the higher reaches of a corporation, organization, or profession, the need for support both within the organization and in personal life only increases. The more lofty your position, the more you need others—contacts, catalysts, sponsors, image builders, and teachers/advisors—to help you achieve your goals. And you require greater technical support to make your personal life operate smoothly.

In order to succeed at this critical point in your life, then, you must accomplish two major goals: You must retain in your supporting cast those who have proven most valuable to you. Second, as you move up, you must reshape your cast, adding members who can help you achieve at higher professional and organizational levels.

As we will see in this final chapter, these two goals are not as easily accomplished as they may seem at first.

THE POST-SUCCESS DILEMMA

Let's look at the first problem you must solve as you move up the professional and career ladder: keeping the supporting cast you already have. To maintain yourself at your new lofty heights and scale ever greater ones, you must retain valuable members of your coalitions and alliances.

At first glance, this might seem a fairly simple task. After all, doesn't success act as its own source of attraction? Doesn't the person who is doing well almost naturally serve as a beacon to those around him or her?

Paradoxically, the more successful a person is, the more difficult it may be to keep many of these coalitions together. I call this phenomenon the post-success dilemma. As we move up the hierarchy, we actually have as much chance of losing our supporters as retaining them. The causes of this dilemma emanate from our own attitudes and actions as well as those of the people around us. Let's look at the roots of the post-success dilemma, in order to develop some strategies for overcoming this career-blocking phenomenon.

The ability to attract and retain supporters is based in part on our personality and how we relate to those around us. To maintain a close circle, we must continue to exhibit the characteristics that made us attractive in the first place: self-confidence, a high sense of esteem, and the ability to appear to be a winner.

But something strange happens to some of us as we begin to succeed. Mid-stride, we begin to falter, losing the self-confidence and sense of command that attracted many of our supporters in the first place.

The results of this loss of self-confidence can be deadly. Our own self-doubts are quickly sensed by others as a sure signal that we are insecure, unsure of ourselves, confused. In business, as in life, this type of image can undermine our attempts to remain attractive to our supporting cast.

Underlying Causes of Self-Doubt

What triggers this self-doubt? There are a number of common underlying causes that my upwardly mobile respondents have reported. These mechanisms are often unconscious. But whether you are conscious of these feelings or not, they will be real in their consequences.

"I really don't think I can handle all this." Many of us have no problem living the life of an average achiever. We don't threaten others, and we are comfortable with their expectations, which we can easily meet and surpass. But as we begin to succeed, we become the admired ones—the role models, the persons others approach with their problems.

While some people thrive in this new position, some of us find ourselves plagued with insecurities we never knew we had. Of course, this is what we wanted, what we've worked so hard for all these years—power, influence, and success. But the risk and responsibility inherent in assuming a lofty perch, and staying there, may scare us to death. We may suddenly be consumed with the fear that we can't meet the deadlines, responsibilities, pressures, and demands of the new management position, the starring role in the play, or the leadership of our own company.

People around us will be quick to pick up on our discomfort. If they feel that we don't have the confidence to perform in our new position, they will not want to remain our supporters.

"I don't deserve this success." Many of us, although we have the talent to handle a new position, seem to be haunted by guilt about our newfound success.

This guilt may have many sources. We may feel that we really don't deserve this success, that luck had a great deal to do with our getting chosen for the new job. We may even sense that we achieved success by default, that there were no truly capable people around to fill the position or get the contract. Worse, we may feel guilty that we succeeded while others around us didn't. This feeling is quite common among those who are promoted directly over peers struggling to achieve their own goals, particularly if these people are personal friends.

If we are surrounded by a sufficient number of esteem builders to remind us that our success is well-deserved, the guilt will quickly subside. If not, these feelings of guilt may interfere with our ability to function, and hence make it difficult for us to retain members of our supporting cast.

"It's all going to end." Some extremely successful people spend much of their time looking over their shoulder. They fear their success is only temporary—that any moment everything could come crashing down like a house of cards. This feeling of impending doom is usually in indirect proportion to how great their progress has been. The lower down the hierarchy they started, the greater their fear that they will lose it all.

Such fears have unhinged many a career. We can't maintain the level of self-confidence necessary to continue to succeed if we are haunted by a sense of impending tragedy.

"My life is going to change." As soon as people begin to succeed, they realize that certain aspects of their lives will change. They may have to adopt new ways of acting, thinking, and dressing. They may have to travel more, take on more responsibility, and reduce their amount of socializing. Moving up, for all its perks and privileges, entails many changes.

Questions abound for the newly successful person: Will my personality change? Will I lose my friends? Will I become a snob? Will I have to act differently and assume a new style of dress? Will I be able to stay "who I am"?

Be assured that such concerns are not uncommon. But they must be confronted and controlled. If you allow your personal fear of success to show, you may lose supporters and become prey to corporate sharks and saboteurs. Remember, your own comfort with your success will go a long way in determining how much support you will get from others.

Others Also Must Adjust to Your Success

The post-success dilemma not only involves how you yourself feel about your success but also includes the way others perceive you. Those around you may have as hard a time adjusting to your success as you do. You must be prepared for the variety of reactions to your success that others—even close friends or supporters—might have. And you must learn to deal with these responses.

·You expect friends and supporters to celebrate your success and continue to remain part of your close circle. You are naturally puzzled as you move up to find your supporters increasingly distant. "What have I done wrong?" you may ask.

The answer is probably "nothing." But nonetheless you need to understand why some people may at least temporarily become aloof or withdraw support.

Here are a few of the reasons why some people who were pulling for you, both in your personal life and your career, may now change their attitude and no longer appear to be sitting in your corner.

They may have trouble relating to the "new you." Your new job entails new responsibilities and status; even the way you spend your time is different. Some people will automatically assume that as you move up, you will move away from them. They may sense snobbishness where it doesn't exist, aloofness where you didn't intend it. You may not be able to see friends as much as you used to simply because your schedule becomes busier and busier, but they may interpret your behavior as a sign that you are becoming estranged from them.

As you move up, in your organization and in your career in general, your lifestyle does change. Upward mobility can have a dark side, marked by a process whereby people become disengaged from their former peers as they move up the corporate ladder. One manager described how his socializing has altered since his promotion:

> Success changes your relationship with your fellow workers on the job, and certainly on the social front. You're no longer palling around with them, and your wives may not be as social with one another as they were.

It is up to you to make others adjust to the "new you," and to reassure them that your relationship will remain close. Later we will look at some of the strategies you can adopt to reassure others that while your position has changed, you haven't.

Your supporters may resent your success. Some of your supporters may quite simply fell threatened, jealous, or even embittered by your success—success that, ironically, they helped you achieve. Perhaps you succeeded too fast, or moved up higher than they would like. You may have taken a position they feel they deserved.

The possibility of resentment looms even larger if you end up becoming a supporter's boss, according to one executive:

> One of the big problems is that the people who were your peers no longer see you as a peer. Now you are making decisions about their careers, and your relationship will never be what it used to be.

This jealousy or resentment should not be ignored. Not only can it ruin your relationship but it can also hinder further career advancement.

"How can I know someone as successful as you?" As you become increasingly successful, you may be surprised that some of those in your social and professional circle have difficulty believing that they know someone as successful as you. A strange response, but one that you will confront the higher you progress in life.

Your current supporters, perfectly comfortable with their image of you as mildly competent, may be having a hard time accepting the fact that such average persons as themselves are now regularly in the company of someone moving up so rapidly in life. Of course, it is not your fault that some supporters feel this way. Their own weak self-image is the root of this problem.

A person harboring such feelings will react in one of two ways. He may abandon you, in which case he is no longer a member of your supporting cast. Or he may remain in your circle, never quite believing that you are improving and succeeding. In other words, he will not fully accept your success. Even if you have grown in skill, depth, and experience, he cannot exorcise his image of the "pre-success" you.

If too many of your old circle cannot support your new identity, you may be in trouble. Their lack of support can have deleterious effects on your self-esteem, and hence your ability to enjoy continued success. You may even "catch" their negative attitude and begin to lose self-confidence.

Listen closely to the statements others make about you and your new position. Do their comments seem to betray an impression that they are more than mildly surprised that you made it? If so, they are continuing to cling to an image of you as just average. Be careful! They may never accept your success.

They may fear losing you as a friend. Some of your supporters, though they may be happy that you are doing well, may fear that your new success will mean an end to your friendship. They fear losing a valuable friend, supporter, even mate or lover. Because they sense that they will lose you, they may gradually withdraw from their role as celebrator, cheerleader, or technical supporter. From their point of view, the more they help you succeed, the more distant you may become.

You may credit their low enthusiasm to resentment or the other reasons previously mentioned. But consider whether it could be fear of the loss of your love that is causing them to withhold support.

These are some of the reasons why current supporters may withdraw from the roles that you have depended on. I am not suggesting that these reactions are in any way inevitable. There are many actions you can take to ensure that you will retain valuable members of your supporting cast and recapture those supporters you may be in danger of losing.

KEEPING THE SUPPORTERS YOU HAVE

You must maintain your bedrock of support. Even though you may need new supporters and may be enlarging your social networks, you must maintain your old ties and strengthen your roots. Your old supporters help you retain a sense of identity.

Losing your supporting cast as you move up can be devastating. We see countless examples in the media and in our own circle of the chaos that ensues when a person becomes disconnected from his or her roots.

To ensure your continued success, you must find ways to solve the post-success dilemma: how to keep the supporting cast that has gotten you where you are. You must discover how to show these people that you still consider them your peers, or at least part of your team.

The following suggestions should help.

Maintain Contact

One young entrepreneur I interviewed revealed how he keeps up his relationships with old school friends, even though he has dramatically outdistanced them in status and income. Once a year, he and his buddies meet in the country for a weekend of reminiscing and general carousing. This provides him with a sense of stability, a continuity with the past.

While you must change some of your affiliations to adapt to your changing situation, if you completely separate yourself from your original support system, you may begin to lose your grip on your new position or power. If you maintain contact with your roots you will have a sound psychological support base from which to move ahead.

Lorraine, an actress, regularly returns to members of her old support system whenever she is haunted by feelings of self-doubt. If a casting call or rehearsal delivers a crashing blow to her ego, she seeks out some of her former teachers from acting school at NYU. These professors have always believed in her talent, and it takes only a half-hour discussion with one of these old esteem builders to get her back on the road to self-confidence.

Some executives stick to their roots by refusing to bow down to one of the cardinal rules of upward mobility: acquiring a new upscale address along with their new job to show that they are "making it." Instead they stay in their old neighborhoods long after they could have moved into richer digs, mainly because they don't want to lose connection with their roots. This gives them a sense of connection to the past, shows close friends and neighbors they are valued, and allows their spouses and children to cultivate their own support networks.

Make an effort to maintain regular social contact with the people who were part of your earlier supporting cast, even if your interests have diverged from theirs. Socialize with them, have lunch with them, do any of the dozens of activities you might do with someone who is a regular member of your social circle.

In a recent *Ms.* magazine article, entertainer Bette Midler revealed the poignant changes that take place in relationships after the achievement of success. According to Midler, success can be overwhelming. People pursue relationships with a famous person, but their motivation is often a bit questionable. Therefore, she goes out of her way to keep up contact with her early supporters. The people she's most comfortable with, she says, are "the people I've known the longest . . . whom I've worked with in shows—musician friends I knew before I was famous."

You must maintain your roots by staying connected to your old friends and supporters. Also, be sure to keep your early supporters up-to-date on what is going on in your life. Don't let your new experiences remain a mystery to them. Let them know that although you have moved up, you still care about them; your values have not changed. Most important, be conscious of any behaviors on your part that might suggest to others that you are becoming aloof.

Let People Benefit from Your Success

Frank Shrontz is chairman of the huge Boeing aircraft conglomerate. He worked himself up from the bottom, becoming president of the Boeing Commercial Airplane Company in 1984, and president of the whole company in 1985.

Very often, when someone ascends to the top of a corporation, those rivals who were passed over for the top quit. But not in this case. Shrontz was able to keep these valuable employees because he convinced them that although he beat them out, they would all benefit career-wise if they stayed on. His success, in other words, would help their careers. They see him as a problem solver, fair-minded, and a good supporter in his own right.

Contrast this with the situation of Peter Cohen, the new chairman of the Shearson financial brokerage. According to an article in *Business Week,* Cohen became embroiled in a series of personality clashes with his top managers, many of whom had helped the company achieve success. According to people inside the company, Cohen isolated some of these managers from key deals and negotiations. These valuable supporters— financial wizards all—felt slighted and left for better positions elsewhere. The question around Wall Street is whether Cohen as chairman can continue to maintain profits for Shearson without these top managers.

As Frank Shrontz's experience demonstrates, the best way to retain supporters as you move up is to allow them to benefit from your success. You must let the members of your supporting cast know that you are looking out for them and are willing to help.

This shouldn't be too hard. As you become more successful—in your career as well as in your life—you have more commodities to bestow upon your supporting cast. You can use your increased power and influence to help the people who "knew you when."

A good example of this type of commodity is information. As you move ahead you gradually acquire more useful information about corporate policy and plans, as well as about your industry in general. As a result you can become a source of information to those around you.

Another commodity you can use to benefit your supporters is power. As an upward-bound manager who wants to retain the loyalty of a supporting cast—co-workers, subordinates, secretary—you must let each of them know that whenever you are promoted, they too may be promoted. They must know that you will move them up when you can, or at least will provide the exposure—within the organization or the field—that will make their advancement possible. In other words, let them know you won't abandon them as you move up the corporate ladder.

Be a Graceful Winner

Supporters won't care how much your success can benefit them if you suddenly start acting superior to them. If you want to keep the supporters you have, you must demonstrate that you are accepting your newfound success with genuine style and grace. If you don't, you might feed into people's natural tendencies to become jealous of your success.

Commonsense behavior will almost assure you of reducing the chances of this happening. For one thing, don't lord it over others, making them feel humiliated by your accomplishments. Not that you should be overly humble. Rather, emphasize the amount of hard work you put into getting where you are and how difficult it is to stay there. You can't make people think that the reason you made it and they didn't is because you are smarter than they are.

Most people who move into positions of power, or become successful in the arts, maintain a service-oriented profile. They make it clear to their supporters, through their actions and attitudes, that they have striven to reach this higher level in order to help others, the company, and society—not to amass glory and wealth.

Remember, as you become a winner in any situation, it is your obligation to keep the networks alive between you and those you are passing by. Always check to see how the people who "knew you when" feel about your success. If their support is waning, it may be because you have developed an insufferably superior attitude toward them, a demeanor that may be laying the groundwork for eventual sabotage by former supporters.

One way to decrease your chance of developing such an attitude—and hence losing your support—is to periodically remind yourself of who helped you achieve success in the first place. Acknowledge that you have a moral obligation—to the cheerleaders, esteem builders, financiers, and others whose support underwrote your climb up life's ladder—to remain loyal to them and help them where needed.

Stay Comfortable with Your Success

So you feel guilty about your own success? Are you in a state of shock that you actually got to this point? Do you fear the new responsibilities that face you in your new position?

If the answer to any of these questions is yes, then beware. Your discomfort, if sensed by those whose support you want to retain, can actually drive even your most ardent supporters out of your cast. After all, how can they adjust to your success if you yourself seem uncomfortable with it?

Managers and other highly successful individuals I have interviewed deliver the same message: you can't help your old cast members adjust to the "new you" if you yourself are uncomfortable with your new circumstances. The more secure you appear in your new position, the more quickly your supporters will adapt to your success.

Therefore, you should seriously consider adopting an attitude suited to your new position: you have made it, you have achieved your goals—now relax and enjoy your new position. Think of the perks and rewards. Why not bask in the glory instead of looking over your shoulder? Why not learn to feel comfortable with the position and power you strived so hard to attain?

People who do not let themselves enjoy the power and success they have achieved run the danger of sabotaging themselves. They look for ways to fail, to remove themselves from the pedestal they worked so hard to ascend.

Don't become your own saboteur!

EXPANDING YOUR SUPPORTING CAST

While it is important for you to keep the supporters you have, you must also expand your supporting cast as you move up, for several critical reasons.

For one thing, new supporters, not having known you before you became successful, may tend to be more comfortable with the new you than your older friends are. And by surrounding yourself with a supporting cast that accepts your success, you may find it easier to adapt to your new status and changed image.

Besides needing people to support your self-image, you may also require an expanded cast to help you adjust to the more complex demands of success. As most executives have learned, the higher up you go, the more precarious your position. You will need new contacts, advisors, teachers, and catalysts.

If you surround yourself only with those who "knew you when," you could be severely hampered in making more forward progress. Of course, you must sincerely try to retain your old supporters even while expanding your cast. Do all that is necessary to make them part of your success. But if some of them can't adjust to the new you, you must break free of them as you expand your cast in new, more positive directions.

The following are a few suggestions on how you can expand your circle as you move up.

- Keep your eyes and ears open to observe potential new members for your supporting cast. Look for the powerful people at your new level who may become your new supporters. Remember, life only gets more complicated the higher you go; the people who survive are those who attract and maintain a supporting cast capable of helping them navigate their way through the unsettled waters of life.

- In any company, you must recruit many of your new equals into your expanded supporting cast. At first, downplay your ambition, and make sure everyone at the new level knows you are there to contribute, not to grab glory from them and usurp their positions. Then figure out how you can help them achieve some of their goals. Let them know that you want to be part of their team.

- At each stage you must show that you are worthy of the position you have just assumed. You don't want to come across as the new kid on the block who has little talent. Look for unassuming forums—staff meetings, for instance—in which you can demonstrate your abilities in a nonthreatening way.

- Practice the "politics of inclusion" with subordinates and anyone you think might resent your success. Make them part of your supporting cast even though your position clearly demonstrates that you hold power over them.

Keep in mind that while you don't want to abandon old friends, there are some roles that your past supporters may not be able to fulfill. If you want to reach your maximum potential, in life or in an organization, you must continually rebuild and reshape that supporting cast.

BEGIN NOW TO BUILD YOUR SUPPORTING CAST

By now, you should recognize how strongly other people influence your life, and in what ways. More important, you have some valuable tools for attracting the people who can help you meet your goals.

Unfortunately, too many people read books like this and then do nothing. They know what they should do, but they procrastinate, unable to overcome their own inertia. Often they just don't know how to make the first move; they don't know how to go about establishing those first connections.

If you are serious about forming a supporting cast, you should begin now. Make it happen immediately, in your job and in your life. Establish an action plan you can use, over the next few days and months, to build your supporting cast. Follow some of these suggestions and you will be on your way to winning with people.

Inventory your needs. Until you know what really makes you happy, it is hard to ask others to help. Therefore, the first critical step in your new program is to understand what you really want from your life and career. In Successercize 1: "Goal Inventory" (Chapter 1) you evaluated a fairly broad range of values and goals. Look over your responses. Which are the goals most important to you?

Take a bold look at your past. Before you can understand your needs fully, you must look at the early influences in your life. Use Successercize 3: "Assessing Your Past" (Chapter 4) to get a clearer view of whether your parents, teachers, and childhood experiences properly prepared you for achieving your goals.

Assess your current social circle. Review the early chapters, especially Chapter 2, "The Roles People Play," to understand what roles are currently being filled in your life and by whom. You will come to an understanding of who and what you require to begin filling your supporting cast needs.

Assess your relationship with your mate. Honestly assess the amount of support you are receiving from your mate. There are some roles that a mate can play better than any friend or colleague. Is your mate fulfilling the support roles that you'd like?

Inventory your strengths. Assess what commodities you have to exchange with others. You will probably be pleasantly surprised at how much you have to give others.

Locate prospective supporters. Begin to look at those in your social and professional circles in terms of the support they might deliver to you. What roles could these particular individuals play in your life?

Be honest with yourself about sabotage. Heed well the earlier discussion of sabotage in Chapter 6. Ignoring the negative influence of others will imperil your ability to reach your maximum potential. Who in your immediate circle either intentionally or unconsciously subverts your self-esteem or undermines your attempts at achieving your goals?

Make your move! As quickly as possible, you should begin to take those actions necessary to recruit members into your supporting cast. Present a report, talk to a friend, ask for support. Take positive steps, like those in Successercize 4: "A Short Visibility Workshop" (Chapter 5) to increase your exposure to potential cast members.

Contribute to others' growth. Consider ways to contribute to others' success as a way of recruiting them into your supporting cast. Look at others' needs in much the same way you analyzed your own. Do your strengths correspond to their needs? If they do, make a concerted effort to join the supporting casts of those you want in yours.

Most important, periodically review this book to reassess your needs and your current cast. You might find it useful to begin keeping a journal to record what actions you want to take to gather supporters. Another useful step would be to periodically jot down lists of the roles you need and who does, or could, fill them—as suggested by Successercize 2: "The Support for Your Life" (Chapter 2). You should also note who is a potential saboteur or image subverter. Such a journal will help you approach cast building more systematically.

Life offers many opportunities. To succeed, you must make the most of them. You don't want to face yourself at middle or old age and look back on a lifetime of unrealized goals.

The lessons of this book regarding success are really simple: You must set high goals for yourself and realize that you have the power to shape your future. Once you set your goals, you need to engage others in helping you on your path. To be a winner, you need other people. Rather than striving as a solitary individual, you can reach your goals much more quickly by enlisting the help of others and giving help in return. Assemble your cast, and be prepared to bring them with you to the heights. Life is, when all is said and done, a cooperative effort.

You have a vision, a dream. Now all you need is a supporting cast to help you realize it.